The Johnny Adams Story

New Orleans Blues Legend

By Judy Adams

Website at www.johnnyadams.org

Printed in the United States of America

First Printing: May 2008

ISBN: 978-0-6152-1394-1

Table of Contents

PROLOGUE

Are you ready for a story that will inspire and entertain you as well as anger and frustrated you all at the same time? Well this is that story. It's about a man, his music and his fight for justice in a music industry that picks and chooses who they play fair with and who they don't. Throughout this book you will marvel at the shear audacity of some of today's biggest labels as they continue to cheat a great artist and his family out of the compensation rightfully and legally due them. Let's find out how they did it and continue to do it even today. Let's start out by talking a little bit about success. It's the American dream, right?

To figure out early in life what your God given talents are and then to find passion in the way you live out your life. The pursuit of happiness, family and success. If you work hard enough and are great at what you do, then success is a given...right? Well, perhaps not always.

The Johnny Adams story is one of passion, talent and great success to be sure. It's the story of a man who made his mark in the world of music though his voice and the songs he sang to a nation. While his story will inspire and amaze you, it will also shock you at times. How can a man with so much success, who's sold millions and millions of records over the years, end up broke, broken and some might say impoverished during the twilight years of his life?

The answers to questions like these are never simple, but for many talented and amazing black artists the realities of a music business wrought with deception and bent on stealing, manipulating and down right lying to these trusting souls, is quite a different thing.

Through the course of this story you will discover that all is not what it seems in the world of music and big business. Even in this present day, Black Artists and their families are being robbed of what is rightfully theirs. Records sales are being manipulated, royalties withheld and talents exploited for personal gain. Taken a step further, it's clear that Slavery is alive and well in much of the music industry today. For Black Artists such as Johnny Adams, this unjust reality has cost him and his family everything.

The American dream…work hard and reap the spoils of your labor…that is unless you happen to be a highly gifted Black jazz and rhythm and blues singer named Johnny Adams. This book will inspire you and enrage you. It will make you laugh and it will make your cry. In the end, our prayer is that this book will make you understand. Help you to see that some of our most loved and gifted musical prodigies are being abused, cheated, manipulated and forced to work for free and sometimes even die broke as a result. Slavery is alive and well in much of the music business for black artists, and it's got to stop. Come follow the story of one such man and his music and learn how a corrupt and racist music business is robbing our musical legends of everything they were, are, or ever will be. This is the story of Johnny Adams; the man, the myth and the legend.

Now a little about the artist. Johnny Adams was one of the last of the great blues and ballad singers of his time. He was an artist who could virtually sing all styles of American music. He was truly an entertainer's entertainer and this was apparent as so much of his shows dripped with the traditional styles of entertainment that included vaudeville along with many other styles.

On occasion, Johnny would pretend to play the trombone, or he would whistle…and boy could Johnny whistle. He would also tell jokes from time to time as part of his show. But of course everybody came to hear Johnny's singing which was flawless; he could sing in the gospel traditions with extraordinary feeling or instantly switch over to jazz with a seamless tone and flavor that drenched your soul with his amazing talent.

Adams actually began his singing career in his hometown of New Orleans working with a gospel group, the Soul Revivers. In the mid-1950's, Johnny would sing alongside Bessie Griffin and her Soul Consolators, but he really made the transition into secular music while singing in a bathtub if you can believe that. His upstairs neighbor, Dorothy

Labostrie, a songwriter, heard his version of "Precious Lord," and persuaded him to sing one of her songs, "Oh Why," It was shortly after that he signed on with the local Ric label.

His first session was produced by Mac Rebennack, 18, later known as Dr. John; "Oh Why" and was released as "I Won't Cry" It became a big hit record in New Orleans for Johnny.

It seemed that from then on, until Johnny signed on with Rounder Records in 1983, he worked in inequitable anonymity and seemed hidden from the mainstream. The control of Johnny's career was in full motion and it would be years and years before the full effect of such stifling power in his life would be felt.

Johnny's singing had a melodic sense of leisure and a seamless train of notes that were unending. He attacked and re-created melodies in ways seldom heard, sometimes leaving them simple and alone, or charging them up with falsettos and other gospel filigrees.

Sadly, by the time all of Johnny's talent had come together, jazz and sophisticated blues singers weren't much in demand anymore. He had small local hits, and one national success with "Losing Battle"; and it was widely reported that Berry Gordy Jr. at Motown wanted to sign Johnny, but like a plague that seemed to follow his career around from almost the beginning, his record company threatened to sue and once again, Johnny's future was controlled and manipulated by the powers that be.

In 1983 Adams began recording what became a nine-album series for Rounder and created tunes that have become jazz standards, like "Come Rain or Come Shine" and "Teach Me Tonight." He recorded "One Foot in the Blues," an album featuring Dr. Lonnie Smith on the organ. At the time this connection with Rounder, along with an increasing and long overdue public appreciation, made him an international concert star and everybody seemed to love him.

Some of the things written about Johnny Adams over the years to describe his talent have been both gracious and heartfelt. It's been said that there isn't a song that Johnny Adams touched that he couldn't turn into gold. Johnny's style was even compared with that of David Ruffin and Billy Eckstine at times. The New York Times once declared that Johnny was able to interject both life and death into every song as he moved from shouts to quivering phrases without effort. A favorite was that every note he sung was as heady as the new car smell in a Cadillac.

CHAPTER ONE

The Real Me

From the instant the melodic voice of Johnny Adams broke the drought silence of a people starving for heroes, this man's honey-rich tones seemed to drip with New Orleans culture and his mere presence with Southern pride.

If you listened very carefully, you could almost hear the essence and origins of New Orleans interwoven within Johnny's own personal history through the words and tones of his heartfelt songs. The same songs he so artfully crafted and spun with a master's touch for his adoring listeners.

Whether singing sophisticated jazz, plaintively hollering in a deep blues groove, or inducing tears with his tender yet emotional spirituals, this talented black artist held his audiences' attention with his rare passion for the music and enthusiasm for life. The Washington Post once said that "Adams combines the forcefulness of David Ruffin with the elegance of Billy Eckstine." A combination that could only be heard in the vocals of this extraordinary rhythm and blues artist.

So who was Johnny Adams really and how did it all start? How was this exceptional talent cultivated and who was responsible for its introduction into the music world of Jazz and Rhythm and Blues?

It all began on January 5, 1932, when Laten John Adams was born in the middle of the music-rich delta of New Orleans Louisiana. Johnny was the oldest of 10 children and was quickly recognized as a gentle and loving spirit. His young and impressionable ears were quickly molded by the cultural heritage of his neighborhood. Gospel, blues, jazz, pop, country and countless other styles whirled around this young man's life from Hollygrove, just west of the French Quarter. This region of the world seemed to flourish with talent and his arrival into this world simply added one more name to the number of exceptional musicians who would flourish in New Orleans. Johnny's musical career began almost from the day he was born and would span another 40 years.

Hollygrove was a low-lying area that sat back a bit from the Mississippi River. This region was extremely prone to flooding and in the late 1920s further precautions were taken to deter rising waters. This area was developed into a working class neighborhood that would become home to Johnny's family in the 1930s. There weren't a lot of jobs

available in Hollygrove back then unless
you worked at the country club or for the
golf course that snaked its way through
the impoverished neighborhood.

      This lack of employment
opportunities forced many of the men who
called Hollygrove their home to travel
miles downtown looking for more
substantial work. The majority of
Hollygrove residents in the 1930s made an
honest but meager living as doormen, store
clerks, or cleaning people in other parts
of this blistering town.

  When Johnny and his siblings were
growing up in the thirties and forties,
Hollygrove was a jumbled up mix of
nationalities and backgrounds. Johnny's
brother, James, remembers vividly that
Hollygrove back then was a neighborhood
not much unlike the Africa of today. The
houses that made up the fabric of this
city were as diverse as the people who
lived in them. If you traveled down one

block you might find tiny, lower middleclass homes stretched out against the horizon like a blanket of un-wanted timber while just a few blocks away you would see sprawling mansions, manicured lawns and realize quickly that the line between rich and poor was clearly defined by street signs and divided by pavement. Although there were no distinct economic or racial splits visible to the naked eye, it was what you didn't see that stuck out like a sore thumb.

This area of New Orleans looked unbalanced in the way homes and neighborhoods were developed…as though you took all of the various puzzle pieces of society, tossed them up into the air and let them land in a haphazard pile that could only be described as mindless.

There were Italians, Germans, black people, white people, Jews, Christians and even a woman who practiced Voodoo living in these neighborhoods. Everybody, especially the children pretty much steered clear of the Voodoo lady, who was not the friendliest of neighbors and could seemingly call up the demons from hell to exact vengeance on anybody she didn't like.

It was a time when superstition and music went hand in hand and everybody who lived in Hollygrove seemed to be comfortable living side by side with their neighbors. It seemed liked everybody there was part of a community family and always strived to take good care of each other.

But just below the surface of a city that seemed to ooze with brotherly love, there were a few invisible barriers within Hollygrove that defined the racial tensions and prejudice that were always prevalent. Black and white children played together happily all day long on these streets and of course the mothers collectively kept their eyes on them.

However, a black child was never permitted into the home of a white child and vice versa. It was an unwritten rule, a law of the land that if not followed, could have dire consequences. When the dinner bells rang, kids seemed to separate like oil from water as they quickly return to their own homes. A black went one way and whites the other without the thought of ever sharing a meal let alone a home. James recalled that for some reason the Jewish families were different. "We didn't even think of them as white people," he recalls, "because their doors were always open, and there were no invisible boundaries to their homes." He remembers a kindly old Jewish woman named Miss Schaeffer who was like a grandmother to just about every child on the block. She always talked about the old country with vigor, with a faraway gaze. And with that gaze would always come just the hint of a tear that would form in one eye and find its way skillfully down one of her rosy cheeks. Back in those days Johnny and his siblings often found school assignments to be odd and impractical. It was crazy. A school just a stone's throw down the street from where they had grown up was suddenly off limits. Off limits because somebody decided that that school would be for whites only. Johnny, his siblings and many of his neighbors had to walk five miles or more to a school that would allow blacks to attend. They would do this by crossing the hazardous canal along with a busy and dangerous major freeway. James recalls on many occasions the dangerous sprints in-between traffic he and others would make as they crossed the busy freeway twice a day. There was no overpass or traffic light to protect them, and many of the school children were either hurt or killed trying to navigate their way to a school that would let them in.

James remembers so many kids complaining to their parents about having to make this dangerous trek to their school every day and asking why they just couldn't go to the schools in their neighborhood. And to add insult to injury, the white kids in the neighborhoods were always picked up by a bright and shiny new school bus, even though they only traveled a few blocks to their schools. Every time Johnny and his siblings complained about the way things were, they were quickly met by a parental response that seemed to provide little satisfaction to their innocent and impressionable minds.

The rules never seemed to be quite fair, but none of the kids growing up in Hollygrove recognized the double standards, racism or prejudice at the time. Those labels came later, when many of them had a chance to leave New Orleans and explore other parts of the country and the world. At that time and place in America, it was just the way it was. It was tolerated, along with a host of other large and small injustices that were part of being a black family in the South.

And then there was the sheer size of Johnny's family. I'm certain if you tried to visualize a family with 10 children, images of pandemonium or semi-controlled chaos would quickly come to mind. That wasn't the case with Johnny and his family. First of all, their parents ran a very tight ship. The children were well-behaved for the most part and knew the rules of the household. You'd also have to keep in mind that not all ten kids lived in the same home.

Johnny's father – affectionately called Shorty, due to his small stature – remarried and moved two doors down with his new family. So there were eventually five kids in one home and five in the other, with Florence the Voodoo woman living in the house in between. The family as a whole was close, regardless of divorce and re-marriage, and the children played well together constantly. James remembers that they were not only siblings, but best friends.

There was a golf course right in the middle of Hollygrove, which could have been the impetus for Johnny's lifelong passion for the game. James recalls climbing through a hole in the fence at dusk after the course had closed. He, along with Johnny and a few additional siblings and neighborhood kids, liked to play the 15th, 16th and 17th holes – but never the 18th. It was too close to the clubhouse and the night watchman. He remembers many an evening scrambling back through the hole in the fence as quickly as possible, glancing fearfully back at a watchman who was running after them shooting his pistol in the air as a warning. James recalls those as exciting and fun times; even with the pistol.

Aside from the typical childhood mischief, Johnny and his brothers and sisters were a pretty good clan. Johnny's father, Laten John Adams, Sr., and his mother, Mary Slater, were each strong role models. Johnny grew up in a religious family with a powerful sense of right and wrong. Family and church were at the center of his life, and they shaped the man he would become.

There was only one black church within walking distance in this small town, and the entire family, both households, attended the "Church by the Canal," as they called it. It was there that Johnny first started to cultivate his musical talent, singing hymns and eventually joining several gospel groups. But that probably wasn't where Johnny first started singing.

James couldn't recall the actual day when Johnny started singing. In fact, he doesn't remember a time when Johnny *wasn't* singing…or whistling. Singing, whistling, or "popping" (snapping) your fingers was eventually forbidden in at least one of the two houses, because the constant noise had become an annoyance rather than a pleasure.

Johnny seemed to have been born with tunes in his head and rhythm in his bones. Music followed him wherever he went and he constantly sang and whistled his way through the neighborhood. He sang everything; gospel, blues, jazz, pop songs, or anything else his ears picked up on. New Orleans had always been fertile ground for music, and he was exposed to a wide range of styles in his eclectic neighborhood. He must have been an easy child to find, because of his constant singing and whistling.

Later on in life, Johnny would be referred to as the Tan Canary. Many people believe that was due to his incredible vocal range, but according to Billy Delle of the New Orleans jazz station WWOZ, it is a little known fact that he was given the nickname more for his beautiful whistling than his extraordinary voice.

The other thing that pegged Johnny as a performer early on was the sheer power of his voice. His mother was always pleading with him to quit "hollering." This reprimand came as a shock to Johnny, because he certainly wasn't intending to yell. He simply had no idea how easily his voice carried. He was a born singer who was constantly reminded to tone it down in and around the house.

Johnny's loud voice did not reflect an overbearing or boastful nature. Johnny was in fact a very meek and kind child, and those traits followed him into adulthood. He was a loving person who cared for and cared about everything and everyone. He mostly kept to himself and was generally not the leader of conversation, but he was a great listener. Johnny could keep a secret. He seemed to be a much better listener than a talker, and he didn't pass judgment on anyone who confided in him. He just let them talk.

If Johnny saw someone in need, he would do anything he could to help. His friends and family knew they could always count on him whenever in a bind. He had a very giving nature, and he was a reliable source of comfort and aid when you needed it. Johnny almost never engaged in an argument, let alone a fight. He was much more inclined to be a peacemaker than a fighter. Unfortunately, his gentle nature and small size made him an easy target for area bullies.

Johnny extended his caretaker persona to the whole neighborhood with one of his first entrepreneurial ventures. He was an industrious child and started shining shoes at a fairly early age. The style for men in Hollygrove was to wear what looked like golf shoes, minus the cleats, and Johnny kept everyone's shoes looking like new. He made the rounds every day to make sure the men knew he was available for a shoeshine whenever needed.

James, seven years younger than Johnny, looked up to his oldest brother and often imitated him. He admired his clean and neat appearance, his hard-working nature and his musical talent. James enjoyed listening to Johnny rehearse in the house with various gospel groups. He said that Johnny would astound other members of the group, because his discerning ear could pick out missed notes immediately, even within complicated vocal arrangements.

He used his extraordinary vocal range to sing all parts, pointing out mistakes and singing the correct line back to the offender, whether they were a soprano or a bass. This was not to find fault or put down fellow musicians in any way. Johnny was always a perfectionist and expected the same of his colleagues.

Today James lives in California. He is a retired Navy officer and firefighter, but he admits with a smile that he has a guitar and piano in his home to "fiddle with," just as he used to when he imitated Johnny as a young man. Johnny was always banging on the piano, picking at a guitar, singing, or whistling. His love of music rubbed off on his younger sibling, and his kind and loving personality had a profound influence on him as well. James always said that Johnny was more like a father figure to him than a loving brother.

Johnny and James not only shared a close relationship, but they occasionally shared jobs. James remembers one of Johnny's odd jobs in a bakery. He lasted about a week and then offered the job to

James. James was looking for some extra money, so he gladly took it. However, he only lasted about a week himself, when he discovered one of his duties was to clean a tremendous stack of pots and pans at the end of the day. Johnny didn't like the job because he hated getting dough under his fingernails. The messiness of the bakery didn't jive with his extremely neat character. James just didn't appreciate looking at that tower of pans to clean at the end of every shift. They both moved on to new adventures.

Another one of Johnny's odd jobs – one that he enjoyed immensely – was as a caddy on the golf course in Hollygrove. He learned the game quickly and became a very good player in his own right. Golf was a life-long passion of Johnny's, and he played often with siblings and friends. I remember him having nine different sets of golf clubs at one time, all with special grips added to his liking. He even tried to teach our daughter and me how to play the game. We had a lot of fun together on the golf course hitting those balls around and trying to do it like Johnny, but unfortunately neither of us shared his talent or his passion for the game.

Even though Johnny's intensity set him apart as an independent child, he was beyond a doubt a momma's boy. A dedicated son who seldom strayed far from home, Johnny spent much of his extra time helping his mother and God was a priority in Johnny's life, even at an early age, but his momma was a close second.

He was extremely protective of his mother, and they enjoyed a close and loving relationship. Johnny's care for dedication to his mother was a thread that ran throughout his life. He spent weeks at a time with his mother in the 1980s when she was ill with a heart condition. We lived in Baton Rouge then, but he would travel to New Orleans and stay with her to make sure she had everything she needed. He bought groceries, took care of her household needs, ensured that she had the medication she needed, and just sat and spent time with her.

I came to love Johnny's mother as well. She was a kind and affectionate mother-in-law to me, and I would have done anything for her. That is the kind of family we were. I felt back then as I still do today, very blessed to be a part of it all. We were always there for each other, and kindness and support were commonplace.

Now even though Johnny and his mother were very close, that's not to say that they didn't have their differences, or that he was a saintly child by any means. He drove her to distraction many times with his extreme neatness. Johnny was very careful about his appearance, in fact he was legendary for that as an adult but even as a child he was very fastidious as well. He would take great care to dress in the morning and if he got the least bit dirty playing outside, he would come inside and change immediately. This exasperated his mother, as she tried to keep up with laundry for all of her children by using nothing but a washboard in the sink! Sometimes Johnny would change three or four times a day in order to stay neat and tidy. His mother scolded him endlessly for using up his wardrobe so quickly and causing her extra work.

Johnny was a small child in stature, just like his father, and unfortunately that brought him a lot of teasing at school. He was called "Bean Pole" and "String Bean," and kids would taunt him and ask him if he needed a sandwich, because he was so skinny. Words were not the only weapons he endured. Neighborhood bullies beat Johnny up more than a few times before and after school. Still, these instances seemed only to reinforce his peaceful nature and build his strong inner self. He didn't retaliate.

One day when Johnny was on his way to school a group of bullies began taunting him. They started throwing rocks and one ill-fated hurl landed a direct hit. Johnny reached up to protect his eye a second too late, and in an instant he hit the ground, bleeding profusely and unable to see. He was quickly rushed to the hospital, but the damage was so extensive he eventually lost his right eye.

Two or three surgeries later Johnny was fitted with a glass eye. The surgeries were painful and headaches plagued him for several months afterward. Unfortunately, his glass eye made him the subject of increased childhood cruelty, and his nicknames went from "Bean Pole" to "One Lamp" and "Oyster Eye."

This experience did not break Johnny's spirit. If anything, the incident strengthened his will and his resolve to be the best at what he did, no matter what the obstacles. Johnny was not a fighter, but he had the strongest resolve of anyone I've ever known. He had Herculean strength on the inside and a cool exterior that never showed an ounce of pain or suffering.

Johnny refused to wear any type of glasses after his eye injury, even though they may have helped to improve the sight in his left eye. Maybe he was tired of the unwanted attention, and he didn't want to give cruel children one more subject for ridicule. He eventually started wearing sunglasses to hide his glass eye.

Most people associate Johnny's signature Ray-Ban sunglasses with his cool, musician persona; however, there was a very real and painful beginning to that fashion trend. His sunglasses became a constant part of his apparel as an adult, to hide his glass eye from the public.

Certainly not all of the attention Johnny received in the neighborhood was negative. There was a woman in the area, who upon hearing Johnny's exceptional voice in passing, immediately told him he should be singing professionally, not playing outside. She ended up giving him a couple of voice lessons, and that set up a discipline of practice that he continued almost until his death. Johnny received no additional formal training, which makes his musical acumen even more astonishing. He practiced on his own daily, fine tuning his musical talent and strengthening his wide vocal range. He knew God had given him an incredible gift, and he worked at polishing it constantly so that it shone brightly.

I don't know if it was the bullying, the long five mile walk to school, or the need to get out into the workplace and make money that caused Johnny to leave school at age 15. I do know that he did not leave school because of a lack of thirst for knowledge. Johnny was an avid reader and continued to educate himself through continually reading books on a wide variety of topics. He was a very good writer as well, as is evidenced in some of the songs he later wrote. His lack of formal education did take a toll, though. He was easily exploited when it came to contract negotiations with record companies. I'm sure that Johnny's early departure from school contributed to his naiveté.

Johnny picked up more odd jobs during the day after he dropped out of school, adding roofer and construction worker to his resume. In the evenings he started singing with a professional gospel group called the Soul Revivers. A gospel group called the Spirit of New Orleans came next. Later on, he joined Bessie Griffin and the Consolators when he was in his early twenties.

He shined in each of these gospel groups and quickly moved to a featured singer role, because his strong voice invariably stuck out in the ensemble. This was an important time period for Johnny's musical evolution because he was able to put his natural talents to work in a professional environment. He sharpened his musicianship and learned what it was like to work with fellow musicians to create a powerful performance. Johnny was known throughout his professional career as a performer that musicians sought out for collaboration, because his rapport with music colleagues was creative and innovative, and his perfectionism produced results with which everyone could be proud.

Johnny didn't stay long in the professional gospel world. His switch from gospel to more popular secular music happened early on and in an unusual way. He was discovered in the bathtub.

Johnny was living in an apartment in New Orleans. As was mentioned before, he sang constantly, day and night. Johnny was actually singing in the bathtub when Dorothy Labostrie, his upstairs neighbor, heard his magnificent voice. Dorothy was a songwriter, known for writing Little Richard's famous tune, *Tutti Frutti*. She knew talent when she heard it. She set out immediately to find out more about the songbird she overheard one floor below her.

Johnny was singing the hymn "Precious Lord, Take My Hand" when Dorothy overheard him, but she eventually talked him into trying out a secular tune she had been writing called "Oh Why." The song name was later changed to "I Won't Cry," and before Johnny knew it, she had talked him into signing with the local Ric label and he was recording his first single.

Mac Rebennack, who was a teenager at the time, produced Johnny's initial solo recording. Mac would eventually be known to wider audiences as Dr. John, and he would be connected to many of Johnny's future recordings.

In 1959, "I Won't Cry" hit the charts, and the young man from Hollygrove saw a bright future in front of him. He seemed to be rocketing toward stardom, as his first recording gave him national recognition. He had high hopes that his musical talent would take him to places he had only imagined and introduce him to a caliber of musicians that he had previously only dreamed of working with.

Johnny would travel the world, and talented musicians across the globe would line up to work with him. But in many ways Johnny's dream fell short. As we explore his life in these next chapters, we will see how Johnny never quite achieved a level of recognition that adequately reflected his talent. His stoic exterior did not outwardly reveal his frustrations, but the hurt was there below the surface, and it could sometimes be heard in the passion of his music. The tune "I Won't Cry" was an eerie prediction of how Johnny held himself up in the public eye as disappointments continued to plague his career.

CHAPTER TWO

Good Morning Heartache

Johnny's early childhood growing up in Hollygrove solidified his strong family ties and rooted his deep faith in God. It gave him a firm cornerstone from which to build the rest of his life. Hollygrove also provided a rich, vibrant, and varied pallet of music and ethnicities that Johnny would draw upon as he built his own musical signature and touched the word with his voice.

A famous writer, Adolph Reed, who just happened to live and grow up in the same small neighborhood as Johnny, Holly Grove, had much admiration and respect for Johnny and his music. So much so that he paid tribute to Johnny Adams by writing about him in his book, "The Color Line W.E. DuBois. That tribute describes how Johnny was able to make it through his music and is a testament to the man and his own unique style and ability to touch so many people with his sound.

That exciting era in New Orleans spawned a large number of talented musicians, writers, and artists. Johnny's smooth, strong and clear sound rings with the echoes of a whole generation. These artists all had important voices that reflected a time in America that one could either be very proud of or very ashamed of depending on your frame of mind. The harmonic honesty in his voice may be one of the reasons Johnny touched so many people with his songs. They could sense the man behind the music and the gift that God wanted him to share with the world.

It became evident early on that Johnny could sing in a wide variety of styles and with an amazing array of sounds. He was comfortable in almost any genre. In 1962 the London Guardian described how Johnny felt that certain music companies tried very hard to stereotype him and his music…he was convinced that their goal was to chain him to a certain sound or specific type of music…the problem was, Johnny's tremendous talent transcended some many boundaries that the notion was impossible.

In the late fifties and early sixties, Johnny's future seemed incredibly bright and prosperous. He had just completed his first recording," Why I won't cry" in 1959 and then later from his first album released in 1969, " A Tan Nightingale" and it was a substantial success, particularly for a previously unknown talent. Johnny was quickly gaining the confidence needed to move forward out of Hollygrove and into the world that awaited him with open arms. Johnny was ready to unleash his talent and share his musical gifts with everybody. Little did he know that record companies and music producers would be ready and willing to take Johnny's music to the next level, but that getting paid for reaching that next level was something entirely different.

That fateful day when Johnny was overheard singing in the bathtub seemed to prove that Johnny was meant to be discovered. His gift was too precious to hide and his talent to valuable to stifle. The Tan Canary needed to fly from home and sing loud and strong, so that all could hear his beautiful voice.

His early foundation gave him the roots to grow from and the wings to fly with confidence. What Johnny didn't realize, and what he would soon discover, was that he did make one fateful mistake. In signing with local New Orleans record producers, his feet were shackled to the very delta that nurtured him throughout his young childhood. Johnny was the artist he was because of where he grew up, but he would have a difficult time reaching the heights he seemed destined for from birth because local producers and promoters seemed bent on holding him down.

Johnny naively believed that the R.I.C. label would lead him into a long and fruitful career, one that would help him to grow and flourish as a musician. In reality, signing with R.I.C was the beginning of a long string of relationships with record labels that seemed to constrict Johnny's talent and hold him back from becoming the artist he was meant to be.

In the late 1950s and early 1960s, Johnny was on the cusp of an international music career. He was building his repertoire, branching out into different genres of music and meeting a whole new group of professional musicians. So what happened? What slowed him down? What stunted his growth?

Joe Ruffino is often given the credit as one of the road blocks to Johnny's success. Ruffino was the owner of the R.I.C. label when Johnny signed with them in 1959, and he held Johnny back in a number of ways. He halted national distribution of Johnny's recordings and he also threatened to sue larger labels that wanted to sign Johnny to recording contracts.

At one point Johnny tried to build on his success and move into the big leagues with a national record label. He traveled to Detroit with several New Orleans musicians to audition for Motown Records. Motown immediately wanted to sign Johnny after hearing his audition. When Ruffino received word of this, he threatened to sue. The chain around Johnny's neck tightened, and he was pulled back to New

Orleans to continue performing primarily for southern audiences.

Another similar event occurred in Chicago. Johnny was performing there, and a representative from Motown caught his show. The new and soon to be extremely successful label tried again to add Johnny to their roster, but it didn't happen. He was literally escorted back to New Orleans and blackballed for several months until he agreed not to sign with Motown. He was told that there would be serious consequences if he ever strayed from his hometown labels.

These instances were not simple contract disputes. Johnny was intimidated, followed, and threatened by small-time labels throughout his career. He feared for his family and his livelihood and he saw no other solution than to continue working with those who held him down and kept his career from taking flight.

When Johnny returned to New Orleans, he had to be extremely careful about the people with whom he chose to associate with and about what he was heard saying in public. He believed that any wrong move would again unleash the wrath of his record producers. If any hint of infidelity got back to the local labels, he feared his career would be over or his family would be in serious jeopardy. These were not just business dealings. They became life and death issues and Johnny was too inexperienced to know at the time that he had retribution, that there could have been an alternative solution.

The bullies of his childhood had returned. Now they wore business clothes and terrorized him by locking him into contracts that paid little money and provided no room for him to attain the level of stardom he so richly deserved.

When Johnny recorded "A Losing Battle" with the R.I.C. label in 1962, the song title seemed to parallel his relationship with Ruffino. And yet, the song was a success. Against Ruffino's best efforts to keep Johnny as a local commodity, the single became a national R&B hit.

Incidentally, "A Losing Battle" was written by the young Mac Rebennack. Johnny continued to cement relationships with outstanding musicians in the New Orleans area, but the mafia-like local labels caged the Tan Canary and kept him from flying very far from his home town.

Johnny was not just the Tan Canary crooning melodious tunes that seem to touch the center of your soul. He had become the canary in the coal mine, warning other musicians not to fall into the same trap. His lack of education and experience kept him in unhealthy relationships with his producers. I hope that by bringing his experience to light, he can now serve as an example to young musicians. My dream is that the Tan Canary will not just be remembered for his beautiful song, but that he will also be lifted up as an example of injustice and a beacon for change.

Ruffino died in 1963, and Johnny was momentarily free, as he was released from his contract with R.I.C. This minor victory turned out to be a short-lived celebration. Johnny repeated his mistake by going from R.I.C. to another small New Orleans label called S.S.S., where he recorded "Release Me" in 1968, and "Reconsider Me" and "I Can't Be All Bad" in 1969.

Johnny bounced around on local labels such as S.S.S. and Ariola for the next several years, going from one bad contract to another, being passed from one producer to the next. His lack of education did not adequately prepare him for negotiating contracts on his own. He was bullied into thinking that he was not allowed to have the kind of legal reinforcement he would need to protect himself from these wolves in sheep's clothing. Johnny did sign with the larger label Atlantic Records during this time, but the period was brief and the union was not a fruitful one.

During this entire period, Johnny was not given a copy of a single contract he signed. I have asked for copies of the contracts from the early days, but none of the record labels are willing to turn them over. As of yet, I have been unable to find valid proof of who owns the masters to most of his early recordings. If these contracts were above reproach, I doubt I would have such trouble receiving copies of them. As of today, I have received nothing, despite numerous requests.

You must keep in mind that Johnny was an easy mark. He was a black man in the South who had dropped out of school at the age of 15. He had incredible musical talent and very little knowledge of the

music business. He had been stripped of
his right to have a lawyer present when he
signed contracts through the forceful
guidance of his record producers. He
didn't have any way of knowing what would
be a fair fee for turning over the rights
to his recordings. He had no idea what
percentage of profits from records sold he
was entitled to receive. It took very
little effort for the record labels to
manipulate Johnny and mentally abuse him
by forcing him to sign contracts he hardly
understood. It was easy to scare him into
remaining under their control.

As I look back at the history of
Johnny's recording contracts, it is
painful to see how they locked up his
talent. When you look at the history in
the light of day, it seems to me like
outright stealing. I wonder why
shoplifting is a crime but this is not? I
cannot fathom how the producers were able
to dine on caviar and steak, while Johnny

sat at home eating beans and rice. It's worse than stealing to take not only money from someone, but to also steal their talent and their potential.

Johnny was never permitted to have his own attorney at signings. He was told that the record companies would "take care of him." Some of the companies played a mental game where they would get close to Johnny and his family – especially his mother. They would trumpet to the world that Johnny was like a brother, but they would hold him to a contract where he received no more than seven cents per album sold.

Johnny was passed from label to label in the local New Orleans scene, and each one used him up and tossed him to the next one. He was paid very little or no up front money for any of his albums and the accounting of his record sales is very shaky. It's heartbreaking to think that Johnny was pouring out his emotions and his talent in recording after recording while these record company owners snatched up his offerings and kept the majority of the first fruits for themselves. I don't think any of them had Johnny's best interest in mind, because not once did they consider what they might do to increase his exposure or further promote his recordings. They just wanted to grab the easy money and discard him.

When Johnny began a nine album series with Rounder Records in 1983, he thought things would finally change. Some aspects of the relationship did change. Johnny was at last with a record label that recognized his talent. Scott Billington pulled together excellent musicians for the recordings. But other than bringing together top quality musicians to work with Johnny, Rounder wasn't much different than the other labels. They still claimed that they would take care of him and made a show of things by visiting his mother and treating him outwardly like a member of the "family."

Nevertheless, when it got down to business, Rounder didn't allow Johnny to have an attorney present at the signing of his contracts, and they paid him almost nothing. Some of the contracts were signed in my kitchen, so I am very aware of the fact that Johnny did not have outside legal guidance or representation. Rounder did not expend much effort to promote Johnny's recordings, either. He remained a local legend with limited outside exposure. Rounder Records, originally of Cambridge, Massachusetts but now based in Burlington, have become very successful over the years. They are an independent record label founded in 1970 by Ken Irwin, Bill Nowlin and Marian Leighton-Levy, while all three were still university students. Rounder is now one of the biggest independent record labels in the United States, with several specialized subsidiary labels. It once served as a major distributor and central sales location for other independent labels specializing in roots music, at one point representing as many as 450 other labels. In the 1990s, though, the company cut back on the distribution effort in order to focus on its own productions. So, New Orleans musicians made a significant artistic contribution to the American music scene in the 1950s and 1960s. Singers like Lead Belly, who emerged in the 1930s, had paved the way. Lead Belly recorded prison songs, folk songs, pop, blues, spirituals, and much more. He was not only a musician, but he was also a historian who documented black history in America.

West African rhythms, military songs, field hollers from plantation days, work songs, hymns, zydeco, jazz, blues, and countless other influences had been mixing together within French, British, African-

American, Spanish, Creole and Cajun cultures for hundreds of years in this fabulous melting pot called NOLA.

It's no wonder that outstanding musicians like Professor Longhair, Dr. John, Fats Domino, Little Richard, Allen Toussaint, Art and Aaron Neville, Irma Thomas, and of course, Johnny Adams, emerged. One would think that New Orleans should have been a major national center for American music recording, with its rich past and promising future. That was not the case. The local record companies just never seemed to get their act together. Chicago, Detroit and Los Angeles took over, and the New Orleans musicians were stuck in the muddy Mississippi delta if they signed local contracts.

New Orleans music thrived in the 1950s and 1960s, which makes it even more unsettling when you think that only a handful of performers reached stardom. Fats Domino, Lee Dorsey and Little Richard were some of those who broke free, but the majority of New Orleans raised musicians remained within the tight grip of local record producers.

Musical innovation was at its height. Professor Longhair had begun putting Caribbean rhythms into his blues piano tunes. Dr. John was combining Jazz, pop, R&B, funk, and rock in ways that no one had heard previously. Fats Domino took boogie woogie, jazz and R&B to create hits like "Blueberry Hill." Johnny was right in the middle of it all, adding his unique voice with all of its textures and emotions.

Aaron Neville worked like crazy in the 1960s, but he remained relatively unknown, because he wasn't provided with adequate promotion to give him recognition beyond the local fan base. Irma Thomas was one of the best soul singers to grace the country at that time, but haphazard material and lackluster promotion held her back.

Professor Longhair ended up working as a janitor after receiving a modest amount of success, because his career stalled. Allen Toussaint collaborated with Art and Aaron Neville to produce groundbreaking recordings, but they were completely unknown outside of New Orleans. Johnny eventually built his reputation more around live performances than record sales, because the producers he hooked up with just didn't have the right stuff.

These musicians were working together, breaking music and color barriers left and right, and building on the history of their ancestors, but the majority of people in the United States had no idea what they were up to at that time. The word never got out.

Johnny recorded a song called "I Wish I Never Loved You at All." At first listen, one would assume he's singing about a woman, but is he?

Johnny soulfully weaves his tune, and these are some of the words that emerge:

> *"I'm not the fool that I used to be…Pain will make even blind eyes see…you're cast aside…how will you find your pride…I gave you trust…a broken heart is never whole again."*

Could his own life experience have laced these words with feelings on another subject that was near and dear to his heart? Did he wish he had never left gospel music? Did he wish he had never signed that first local contract?

Johnny picked songs carefully, and he sang with the pain of a heavy heart that only comes from true life experiences. He was able to produce such achingly beautiful renditions of songs like

"Release Me," "Losing Battle," "My Heart is Hanging Heavy" and "After Dark" because he had his share of heartbreak. But you have to look past the obvious meanings in the songs and peer into Johnny's life to see where the pain really originates. He lost his freedom with some of these companies. They held him prisoner, and only in death were his shackles released but were they.

Johnny was constantly threatened during the early part of his recording career. He was forced over and over again to sign contracts.

CHAPTER THREE

After Dark

Johnny often found himself extremely frustrated by the record producers to which he found himself shackled, but his musical outpouring was never stifled or affected by his personal battles. Rather than giving up, Johnny always chose to concentrate his attention in different areas of the business. During this time in his life, he increasingly turned his attention toward live performances, making a living on what was called the Sugar Cane Circuit.

In the 1950s, when Johnny first began to tour the Sugar Cane Circuit, segregation was just ending and racism was alive and well in the Southern United

States. It was sometimes a hard road to travel and always frustrating, but the music that emerged through Johnny's experiences and travels was astounding. He had the uncanny ability to take life's worst and internalize that into music that showed life's best.

The Chitlin' Circuit, which was a national classification for clubs that would allow black musicians to perform, had been developed years earlier. The venues on the Chitlin' Circuit were instrumental in the careers of musicians like B.B. King, James Brown and Jackie Wilson in the 1950s and 1960s, due to the fact that media coverage was non-existent for minorities. If you were black and wanted more than a handful of family members to see you perform, then this was how that happened…it was the only way that happened. The Chitlin' Circuit referred to black-friendly venues across the country that also offered chitlins and other soul food dishes as part of their regular fare to go along with the excellent music. The Chitlin' Circuit was one of the only ways for fans to be able to hear their favorite African-American musicians in a live performance venue and it quickly grew in popularity.

The Sugar Cane Circuit was really a sub-set of the Chitlin' Circuit. It could be thought of as the deep Southern branch of the network, existing below the Bible belt. The pay was not great, but the musicians who traveled together or met up on the Sugar Cane Circuit produced unforgettable performances and some of the greatest artists of all time emerged as superstars of their day. Johnny's regional hits "Reconsider Me," "Release Me," and "Hell Yes, I Cheated" were favorites in these shows.

Back then black musicians in the South didn't stick to playing in their own neighborhoods. The Sugar Cane Circuit included honkytonks, society functions, concert halls, bars, and even former bordellos across the lower part of the United States. Sometimes Johnny had to enter through the back door of white only establishments, but he grabbed on to the chance to perform and use his uncompromising talent to unite people of all nationalities in common appreciation of the power of music.

Johnny was a born performer, and his concerts drew a large and loyal fan base. Audiences were amazed by his range and his expressive renditions of songs. Johnny was also known for getting into a groove with his fellow musicians and making music into the wee hours of the morning – much to the dismay of a few sleepy club owners. He didn't care if there were only five people left in the club, he would keep going until they turned out the lights.

Sometimes, just getting to a gig on the Sugar Cane Circuit was a dangerous adventure. Towns like Metairie, Louisiana were known Ku Klux Klan centers, and Johnny and other musicians prayed that their cars would not break down as they drove through these areas. Johnny would often leave a day early and stay overnight in a hotel, so that he would not be on the road alone late at night and easy prey for racism.

I remember how hard Johnny worked to scrape together extra money from shows on the Sugar Cane Circuit to buy the car of his dreams. After three years, he finally saved enough money to buy a beautiful white Lincoln Town Car. From then on he traveled in style to performances, with a car that matched his dress code!

Unfortunately, his joy was short lived. About a year after purchasing his Town Car, Johnny walked out to the parking lot after a late final set at a local club in New Orleans, and the only sign of his car was a few shards of glass in the parking spot where he left it. Johnny called me immediately, and I threw on some clothes and drove from Baton Rouge to New Orleans at 2am to bring Johnny safely home. It was a frightening evening, because we didn't know at the time whether or not the vandalism was related to threats from record producers, or if it was a random act. Police officers found Johnny's car about a week later, abandoned and completely totaled.

In spite of dangers and setbacks such as these, Johnny absolutely loved to perform. He summed up the feeling so eloquently in an interview with John Sinclair, who hosted the "New Orleans Music Show" and "Blues & Roots" programs for WWOZ Radio in New Orleans:

"You know, sometimes, man, you sing…one of those songs and look at the expressions on people's faces — you stand up there and look at people in the audience and you can

hear their cigarette ashes hit the floor.
It makes you feel good sometimes, you
know?"

There were many places where Johnny was not welcome due to the color of his skin, but he continued to travel the Sugar Cane Circuit and made sure that his performance, his dress, and his professionalism were beyond reproach. He did not want to give any white business owners an ounce of ammunition against him. He detested the term "boy" that was used so often in the south by whites to refer to black men. So, he chose to combat the racism in his usual way. He did not fight. Instead, he dressed and acted in a way that made the condescending label seem ridiculously out of place.

Johnny's dress and demeanor accentuated and reinforced his colossal talent. He wore Italian suits and silk ties, and he had a closet full of expensive shoes that were always polished. Johnny encouraged his band members to dress well, too, and arrive to a gig on time. He was keenly aware of the fact that the color of their skin gave them an immediate disadvantage in white clubs, so he wanted the band to do whatever it took to make up the difference.

Guitarist and vocalist, Walter "Wolfman" Washington, was part of the band at that time, and he loved Johnny's clothes. The two were like brothers, so Johnny ended up letting Walter have a few of his suits. Walter wasn't a spiffy dresser when they first met, but he picked up on Johnny's style.

In white clubs, Johnny and his fellow musicians sometimes had to enter through the back door. In the black clubs, they could come in through the front door, the back door, or the window. No one cared – as long as he came in and stayed awhile!

Whether Johnny was able to walk in the front door, the back door, or through the window, he did so with dignity and grace. His appearance was impeccable. He wouldn't think of showing up with a wrinkled shirt or with dirt under his fingernails. Then, when he got to the business of his music, he would never disappoint.

Johnny also made the rounds to local New Orleans clubs. Some of his favorites included Tipitina's, the Rock N' Bowl, Dorothy's Medallion Lounge, and Snug Harbor. Each one of these clubs had its own individual charm.

Tipitina's was in uptown New Orleans. Before its doors opened in 1977, the building had been a gambling house, a gymnasium, and a brothel. The logo for Tipitina's boasts a banana, which seems odd unless you know that Tipitina's was originally a juice bar and restaurant, as well as a music club and bar.

Snug Harbor is right in the middle of the Frenchmen Street scene. It is an intimate, cozy venue that includes a restaurant with romantic candlelit tables and a welcoming bar surrounded by dark wood. The performance area is more majestic, with 25 foot ceilings and two levels for audience members to enjoy the shows.

The New Orleans Jazz and Heritage Festival was another highlight of the year for Johnny. Jazz Fest began in 1970, and each year it is a celebration of music and southern culture. Organizers started the festival as a means to highlight and celebrate the birthplace of jazz. It is a time for great musicians throughout the world to come together and commemorate the importance of New Orleans in American music history as well as lift up a rich cultural center that shaped not only music, but also art, cuisine, and southern culture. Johnny was involved in Jazz Fest

from the early years through the final
years of his life.

CHAPTER FOUR

Walking on a Tightrope

Johnny had an amazing gift for finding the gold and glitter in each and every song he sang. He also had an amazing talent for bringing out the very best in people. He always recognized the precious nature of all those around him, and he treated everyone with respect, dignity and kindness, even if the favor was not returned.

I would like to share with you more about Johnny the man in this chapter. His talent as a musician was legendary, but I would like for you to understand more about him as an amazing person. Johnny was not just a commodity, not just a talent, not just an avenue for record producers or big business to make more money off of, he was also a kind and loving man who wanted nothing more than to touch the hearts and minds of all those he ever came in contact with. . He touched the lives of countless friends, musicians, and family members along the way to his success and we have all been changed for the better because we were permitted to share in a little part of Johnny's life.

Johnny always stayed away from gossip, instead choosing to remain positive and uplifting in his typically soft-spoken manner. You always felt a little better about yourself and about the world around you after spending time in Johnny's presence. He always seemed to find the good in people even when it wasn't clearly seen. He disregarded the bad and was a man who never judged a soul.

Johnny would not allow anyone to speak ill of his friends and he would always come to their defense immediately in times of conflict. His spiritual roots and honorable upbringing made no allowance for gossip and insults and Johnny was never one to waste his emotion on anger or revenge. His was a loving and kind soul that transcended even the music he sang. He had a quiet strength that people admired and respected and I think it's one of the things that always seemed to show itself though his music.

Johnny had zero tolerance for violence, even though he grew up in a city where violence and racism were commonplace. He thought that if you disagreed vehemently with someone, you should remove yourself from his or her presence, rather than get into an altercation. Johnny was a peacemaker. I never remember seeing him in any sort of conflict the entire time we were together.

Johnny's peaceful nature turned him into a counselor to his friends and family. He could be trusted not to pass on your personal business, and his levelheaded view on situations often provided solid advice for taking action.

Johnny did not lead a stereotypical musician's life. It wasn't sex, drugs, and rock 'n' roll that kept him going. In fact, Johnny didn't drink alcohol or use drugs at all. His fellow musicians would lightheartedly joke with him about his love of Coca-Cola, which he drank at gigs instead of alcohol.

Fellow musicians often offered Johnny drugs, but his response remained the same. He would smile and say, "I don't need drugs. I'm not sick! Drugs are for sick people." Again, his response was not a judgment, but rather a quiet refusal to participate. He chose a less-popular route, but his quiet inner strength allowed him to follow his own desire to not cause himself any harm.

Johnny firmly believed that drugs and alcohol negatively affected his voice. He took great care of it always, often drinking tea with lemon, juice, and water. A healthy diet that included many fruits and vegetables also helped Johnny maintain his slim, fit appearance throughout life. He understood that the voice his livelihood depended on came to him as a gift from God, so he treated it with great care and practiced daily to stay vocally fit.

The fact that Johnny took particular care of his voice and health without using drugs or alcohol did not mean he was a prude or a killjoy. Johnny's easy-going and loving nature caused him to seek the company of a host of friends and family; he enjoyed his down time just as much as the time he spent making music.

Johnny lived his childhood next to a golf course, and one of his favorite pastimes as an adult was playing golf. Haywood and his other local buddies in Baton Rouge were always up for a game when

Johnny was home from his road trips. They would make modest wagers on the game, and Johnny often won. It wasn't big-time gambling, but they all looked forward to the friendly competition. They bet a few dollars on each hole, and every time Johnny won, he would grin and say, "Look! Money for golf balls!"

Johnny also played a lot of golf with his brother, Alvin. They got together for a game every chance they could when Johnny was back in Baton Rouge. They would go to the LSU Golf Course, City Park Golf Course, or Webb Park Golf Course to play. Johnny kept in close contact with all of his brothers and sisters. Their loving family remained close-knit, even through their adult years. They continued to have fun together and look out for each other, just as they did when they played together as children in Hollygrove.

Johnny participated in a number of local golf tournaments, and everyone wanted him to be on their team because of his skill and easy-going nature. He was a fun person to be around and an asset to the team. He often played in tournaments in Gulfport and Biloxi, Mississippi, and we would bring our daughter Alitalia along for a little play time at the beach.

Alitalia loved to play at the seashore. She would bury Johnny in the sand – usually starting with his face first! Her little hands would fill a bucket full of sand and then dump it right on Johnny's head. Then, she would quickly brush the sand away from his face to reveal his broad grin. I could hear their laughter all the way down the beach as she covered him from head to toe.

Johnny's laid-back attitude also made him a favorite in the recording studio. The casual, fun atmosphere he created at recording sessions gave fellow musicians an opportunity to explore their creativity and try new things. His perfectionism also helped to produce nearly flawless final products. He picked over recordings repeatedly, finding nearly undetectable flaws to fix that escaped most producers' ears.

The music fan can hear an example of Johnny's personality and the studio atmosphere he created in the final track of *The Verdict*, which Rounder released in 1995. On this track, called "D Jam Blues," you can hear Johnny laughing and improvising with Jimmy Singleton and Shannon Powell. The lyrics talk about waiting until 7pm, when one of their favorite restaurants was finally open for business.

Johnny was a loyal friend and a spiritual man; he was a perfectionist and a peacemaker; he was low-key, soft-spoken, and articulate; and finally, he was a man who took care of himself. Nevertheless, there is one more thing I would like you to consider when you look at Johnny the man: he was an unbelievable dresser!

The first time I laid eyes on Johnny, he wore a white suit, and I had never before seen such a handsome vision. Johnny also loved bright colors. He had the most beautiful, brightly colored Italian suits that he wore in performances with exquisite silk ties. As I said before, his shoes were also impeccable. He would fly to New York or California, just to get a good pair of shoes. The man exuded class and sophistication. *Jet* Magazine even took notice of his dazzling style.

Johnny took good care of himself and the people around him. Taking nothing for granted, he seemed to soak in every aspect of life, from choosing a silk tie to sitting down to have a good conversation with a brother or sister. He cherished life and the relationships that he forged along the way.

Johnny was also becoming an actor in his own right. He was in "The Bird" directed by Clint Eastwood and starring Forest Whitaker. Another little known fact about Johnny was that he and Fats Domino were very good friends. He and Harry Connic Jr. were also very good friends as well as Aaron Nevilles and the Neville brothers who were very close to Johnny.

Johnny has to his credit 26 albums, 1 single, 2 soundtracks, Bowfinger, the movie, 1999 by David Newman second original soundtrack (tune in tomorrow) by Winton Marsellis and 114 discography. Johnny always seemed to be surrounded by famous people. He also performed with BB King on several occasions, Harry Connick JR., Bonnie Raitt, Aaron Nevilles and many more famous artists. Johnny song "There's Always One More Time" is the opening song in the Bowfinger movie…you remember the

one starring Eddie Murphy and Steve
Martin.

CHAPTER FIVE

One Foot in the Blues

Family… There was never a doubt in my mind that family was the single most important thing to Johnny. I've touched upon the fact that Johnny grew up in a very close family. For Johnny, the order of things was very simple…God came first, family second and then there was his music. Johnny, all his siblings as well as his parents were always there for each other no matter what; and that was something that Johnny always cherished.

Johnny's mother was his strength his rock. She nurtured him as a small child and continued to give him great advice as an adult as he battled life's challenges and navigated the pitfalls of success.

Johnny took good care of his mother in the twilight of her years by paying for her, helping with her medicine, buying groceries, and spending time with her whenever he was not on the road.

It seemed that strong women surrounded Johnny throughout his life, and his mother was someone special he would always go to for counsel and grounding.   I'd say that the bond between Johnny and his siblings was equally sturdy. I was lucky to have witnessed so many times the way that they were woven so tightly into each other's lives and how they relied on one another in times of trouble and need. They were not just relatives who acted out of responsibility, they actually enjoyed spending time with each other and it showed in everything that they did. They lifted each other up, picked each other up and made sure that love was the binder that held the pages of their life together. I believe that is a rare gift today that unfortunately is not a given in all families.

One incident in particular comes to mind. I remember when Johnny's brother, James, heard that Johnny had been diagnosed with cancer; he immediately flew from California to Louisiana to be at Johnny's side. I was able to bear witness to that steel bond between these brothers. Every day in that hospital, James sat in a chair on one side of Johnny's bed, and I sat in a chair on the other side. We all talked about old times and listened to great music. James probably shouldn't have been traveling himself since he had recently suffered a stroke and had not yet fully regained his strength, but he stayed with us for 2 months…right to the very end.

And it wasn't just in times of need that brought this loving family together.

Johnny thoroughly enjoyed laughing and joking around with his kin. They golfed together, visited each other often and always joked and teased each other in true sibling fashion. This family was truly blessed with the gift of love and caring for each other. When I became a part of Johnny's family in a small wedding ceremony in Baton Rouge, I felt welcomed and loved right from the beginning. But perhaps I'm getting ahead of myself here. Before I get into all that, I would like to recount the day when Johnny and I first met.

We met completely by accident – or some would say it was all part of God's plan to bring us together. I was working in Baton Rouge as a corrections officer and I had just finished a particularly long and difficult shift. A friend of mine wanted me to go to a Johnny Allen concert with her that evening. I was exhausted and didn't really want to go, but she eventually talked me into it. We donned evening dresses, refreshed our hair and make up and arrived at the Hilton in Baton Rouge a bit late, only to find that it was not Johnny Allen, but Johnny Adams who was performing that night – and the band was on a break.

I must admit, I was tired and a bit annoyed when I walked into the crowded ballroom. There wasn't a seat to be had, Johnny Allen wasn't even performing that night and the band that was performing had just left the stage. I crossed my arms and rolled my eyes expecting a dismal evening, but two seats suddenly opened up at a table facing the stage and I thought, well, at least I can sit down and rest a little. My friend pounced on them immediately and we ordered a couple of daiquiris. Maybe the night wasn't a complete loss I thought to myself…things started looking up. I had a few of Johnny Adams' records and I knew he would be an excellent performer; that was if he ever actually got back on stage.

Johnny was actually standing to the left of the stage greeting his fans when we found our seats. He was wearing a beautiful white Italian suit and when he turned around and I looked into his eyes, I finally understood what it meant to be smitten. Suddenly, love at first sight made perfect sense to me. My heart stopped. He was gorgeous and suave. He had a jerry curl, just like Little Richard's. Our eyes locked for a magical moment and he immediately made his way toward our table with a look that said he had been waiting for me all of his life.

I was so happy that I had chosen to wear an evening gown, also in white, elegantly adorned with lace and pearl beading. Now that I think of that night, it's as if a movie director planned everything from the very first scene; from my friend's mistaken identity of the performer, to our matching white attire, to the table that was vacated just in time. It is such a sweet memory that I replay over and over again in my mind's eye.

Johnny arrived at our table and introduced himself. He paid for our drinks. As I thought about that later on and after I got to know the man so well, it was surprising. He was so very careful with his money, but not because he was cheap or miserly. He always saved most of his money for his mother or other family members who were in need, so every penny always counted to Johnny. I remember asking when the band would be starting up again, but the rest of the conversation is a bit of a blur. What I remember most is the fact that we could not stop staring to each other. It was as though we'd known each other for years and years and just has so much catching up to do. After a few more tantalizing moments of small talk, the band assembled back on stage and started playing, but Johnny didn't join them right away. Instead, he asked me to dance. We danced together for a couple of songs, both of us trying to keep control of the butterflies in our stomachs. Finally, Johnny joined the band, but not before he politely asked me to stay until the end of the show so that we could talk more. From that moment on, I became a believer in love at first sight.

After the show, we spoke for a short time and exchanged phone numbers. Johnny said that he was traveling the next day to Kansas City for a performance, but he would like to call me at 4pm, if that would be all right. My first thought was, yeah, right!

As I walked out of the Hilton with my girlfriend chattering on about what a beautiful couple Johnny and I were on the dance floor, I smiled to myself at the magical evening and all the surprises it brought, but I doubted that this traveling musician would ever actually remember to call me.

The next day, at 4pm on the dot, my phone rang. Johnny was a man of his word. We spoke on the phone for 3 or 4 months as he was traveling throughout the United States. When he returned to Baton Rouge, we began our courtship. He was always a perfect gentleman, never saying anything out of line or expecting anything from me. He also did everything he could to protect me from the media, who followed him to performances regularly, by coaching me on how to avoid them. He was very protective and chivalrous.

Even though Johnny had to travel for his livelihood, he was true family man. After we were married, we settled in Baton Rouge. He was a dedicated and honorable husband, and we shared a huge amount of trust between us.

When he worked it was amazing how hard he worked! I respected him for that and I encouraged him to follow his path in music. Sometimes I even traveled with him, but most often he went on his own. He was allowed to travel and have his freedom, and I never questioned him. The trust was there. He could travel wherever his music took him, and I would be home waiting for him. Trust was a fixture, a cornerstone of our marriage.

Johnny would say to me, "Judy, I want to be able to work and travel and come home to a wife I can trust." He trusted me with his life. I was his life, and he was mine.

Johnny's popularity began to grow overseas, and he increasingly traveled abroad to perform. He was just about to board an Alitalia flight to Europe when he called me and I gave him the news he would be a father. I was expecting a baby girl. Johnny was ecstatic, and when our daughter, Alitalia, was born, I discovered another true calling of Johnny's…it was fatherhood. Johnny brought me back a tiny model Alitalia plane after that trip, and we held each other close and dreamed of our new little family.

The birth of Alitalia brought out a new side of Johnny. He was a doting father who spent a lot of time laughing and clowning with Alitalia when he was home. He also started to pass on to her everything he knew, right from the start. I didn't know then that he would be taken from us far too soon; in fact it would be when Alitalia was only seven years old. I'm glad he didn't wait for her to reach a certain age before he started teaching her about music, in particular. He was eager to share his joys with his beautiful little girl, and as it turns out, there was no time to waste.

I can still see Alitalia, just two years old, standing on a little footstool.

She was so tiny and so proud of herself standing before a microphone that Johnny would rig up for her. She loved to practice with him each day, and she sang along with his records. He playfully taught her the vocal tricks and exercises that allowed him to have such a huge vocal range. Then, he would get her to sing songs from his records. "Body and Fender Man" was one of her favorites. It still makes me laugh to think of our little girl crooning into the microphone, having no idea what the words meant, but having the time of her life performing for her daddy. After their singing sessions were finished, Johnny would put Alitalia on his back and crawl all over the house as she giggled with delight. Our house was always filled with laughter and play.

I remember one particular Christmas when Johnny came home with the ultimate gift for Alitalia. It was a bright red tricycle, complete with horn and a basket on the front. You would have thought he won the lottery when he arrived with that gift he had so carefully chosen. Of course, it had to be bright red! He took immense pleasure in giving, and he was always generous to all of us in his family.

Johnny and Alitalia were partners in crime, too. He decided he wanted to teach her how to golf, but he was informed by the manger that children were not allowed on the golf course. That, of course, didn't stop the two of them. Johnny's childhood shenanigans were relived as he and Alitalia snuck out on the course after hours in a golf cart so she could hit balls. When she was around five years old, he bought Alitalia her own clubs with special grips. She liked putting the best. "Puttin' the ball in the hole!" she would cry with glee.

Truth be told, Alitalia probably liked to play with the ball picker-upper more than her clubs, but five-year-olds are easily distracted. The two of them had a wonderful time together out on the green after hours, and Alitalia holds fond memories of that experience with her father.

The three of us played together and laughed together; Johnny taught Alitalia how to sing, to play the guitar, and to golf. Our home life was full and joyful. Johnny was a dedicated and honorable husband and a nurturing father. The time the three of us had together ended far too soon.

I remember when Johnny was bedridden at home in his final months. Alitalia would drop her school bag at the door and climb right into bed with him. They would lie there together all night, singing, reading stories, and talking, and she would fall asleep in his arms. I watched them sleeping and tried to will his cancer from his body. But when Johnny did leave us, he left us with his strength and his strong sense of family. We honor him when we continue to cultivate those gifts he so lovingly put in our hands through his actions and example.

Johnny may not have been extremely successful financially, but he was wealthy. His wealth was in his family ties, in those deep and lasting bonds that gave his life meaning, hope, and joy.

One very emotional time for Johnny was when he and I purchased our home. We purchased a modest three bedroom home in Baton Rouge Louisiana. The house was in a mature neighborhood with a large magnolia tree next to one of the bedrooms. I remember he loved the smell of the magnolia flowers that bloomed in the spring time. The home was located near a local community golf course. As you can imagine, this was a piece of heaven for Johnny. He being such a great golfer this was where he wanted to be as much as possible. I remember that the back yard was very large which was great for cookouts because grilling was something Johnny loved to do, and was good at it. The large garage was where he kept a collection of golf clubs… pings being his favorites. Of course his golf buddies would comment on how sharp they looked, and what a great collections he had. The garage was not only used to store his favorite golf clubs. Johnny would also turn the garage into his music studio. He practiced on his vocals constantly. That was also where he trained daughter Alitalia. In-between shining those golf clubs and setting up his studio, we knew this was truly a home for him. Johnny had now found peace and a little joy.

One year after purchasing our home with very hard work and keeping close track of every penny, Johnny was finally able to purchase the car of his dreams. It was a new Nissan Maxima and it was a beautiful forest green. It certainly matched his wardrobe…brilliant and dashing, oh, and well polished. Yes, this was truly a match made in heaven. No one could have picked a more fitting car. This was a very happy time in Johnny's life he… had a home, a new ca, and finally a little peace which seemed to always elude him. He was truly happy.

CHAPTER SIX

I Only Want to Be with You

Johnny realized early on that he could not earn a living by depending solely on his unfavorable record contracts, and that his meager share of record sales would not always pay the bills. Johnny, the beloved friend and family man, knew that in order to make a living as a musician, he would need to travel and bring his deep reservoir of talent directly to the people.

Therefore, Johnny made a very difficult decision…he would temporarily leave his family and friends behind and tour the world; he would do this for his family and for his fans sharing his love of music with people from all over the globe.

However, if truth be told, Johnny loved performing live, in spite of its costs. He was energetic, entertaining, and always on his game when he took to the stage. Leaving his loved ones behind was a painful drawback for a loving and caring man like Johnny, but a funny thing always happened on the road that he just could never explain…he would became part of a second family, a musical family.

I remember one time Johnny telling me about his friend Walter "Wolfman" Washington, the singer and guitarist who would eventually become his bandleader. When they traveled together or met up on the road someplace, it was like being home for Johnny. And there were others. Whenever he would meet up with additional members of his on-the-road family of musicians, these venues and musical festivals would serve as impromptu reunions. He frequently played with old friends at Jazz Fest in New Orleans, the Long Island Jazz Fest, Austin City Limits, and festivals in Colorado, Kansas City, and California; so it was almost like he had family with him all the time.

Johnny also performed frequently in Japan, Germany, Switzerland, Canada and the United Kingdom. His popularity began to mount in Europe and several record producers overseas encouraged him to move to Europe permanently. The thought was very intriguing for Johnny because he continued to be shackled by local New Orleans record producers that persistently stunted his growth in popularity in the United States. They would have no power over him in foreign countries.

When Johnny brought back the tiny Alitalia plane for me, it was not just a token gift of the joy we shared in my pregnancy, it also represented his dream for us to start a new life in Europe together. We were seriously considering moving abroad right before Johnny became ill with cancer.

European record companies quickly recognized that Johnny was not getting the recognition he deserved in the United States, and they felt they could launch him into a much larger market over seas. Keep in mind that they were not completely selfless in their suggestion. They also wanted to capitalize on his potential for stardom, but the idea of working with producers who recognized his potential rather than crushing it every step of the way was very attractive to Johnny.

I recall that each trip, whether in the U.S. or abroad, added to Johnny's loyal fan base. Johnny was fascinated by the multicultural gathering that would show up at his performances. He would gaze out at a crowd and observe a sea of various colors and backgrounds. He believed his music provided a unifying force to his listeners. Even though Johnny didn't march in civil rights protests, he knew he could use his music to promote unity and equality among races and cultures. To borrow from the words of one of Johnny's heroes, he had a dream. Johnny had a dream that music could bridge the gap and cross over to various sectors of society. His music did bring people together. His dream was realized. Johnny marched with his music.

Johnny was also able to use these venues as a showcase for his astonishing talent. He had very little restriction on the type of music he performed, so he did everything. He sang jazz, blues, country, R & B, gospel and pop. He latched on to what got the best response and altered his show to fit the desire of his audience.

He was quoted in the *Washington Post* (March 19, 1989) after a performance, responding to a question about his wide range of styles:

"I have to live up to all of these names," said Adams. *"It's not that hard though, I just find out what people are boogieing and execute my music to fit their desires."*

Johnny could not be pigeonholed into one type of music. He was a musician -- a great musician! The type of song didn't matter. Through his travels, Johnny had a pulse on what people enjoyed, and he gave them what they wanted.

The ever-increasing Johnny Adams fan base only had one complaint. They could not understand why he wasn't a superstar. His fans guessed that something was holding him back, and they openly wondered what that something could be. Johnny performed in festivals alongside internationally famous musicians, but he had only a fraction of the recognition. Fans witnessed the respect he received from famous musicians with which he performed, and they speculated on reasons why his career did not provide similar achievement.

It was difficult for Johnny to know deep down the talent he possessed and see how he affected audience members when he performed live, but then continually scrape together a modest living. He did so with grace and dignity, and he very seldom let his disappointment show. We talked about it in private, but he never revealed any sort of depression or heartache to his fans. No matter what the record companies did to hold Johnny back, he continued to demonstrate a strong exterior, and he continued to make music any way he could.

Johnny's talent even spilled over into the movies. He added actor to his resume when he was featured as a bartender in the movie *Bird*, directed by Clint Eastwood. The story was about the jazz musician Charlie "Bird" Parker. Johnny was also featured in two videos on musical techniques by drummer Omar Hakim: *Let It Flow* and *Express Yourself*.

Johnny enjoyed his travels, and his reputation and his fan base grew as a result of his hard work on the road. Nevertheless, he continued to be held back by the local record labels. New albums were released periodically, but they were not properly promoted, so they never reached more than modest success. When one listens to Johnny's soulful style, it's obvious that he was intimately familiar with disappointment. He knew what it was like to feel regret and frustration.

CHAPTER SEVEN

Room With a View of the Blues

Johnny's many travels over the years have brought him closer and closer to his fellow musicians. The musical family that was forged on the road was not a loose grouping of people who just happened to work together, they were people who truly cared for one another and looked out for each other in times of need. It was a secure and reassuring feeling for them all, knowing that even on the Sugar Cane Circuit or playing at international jazz festivals, they were never alone.

The musicians were a close knit group and this was particularly true of the crowd from New Orleans. They would spend time together even when they were home and not working. There were studios and clubs all over New Orleans where Johnny and his cronies would congregate to share their creative ideas and practice together.

Aaron Neville, David Torkanowsky, Duke Robillard, Dr. John, Harry Connick, Jr., Dr. Lonnie Smith, and Houston Person. They all worked together and took care of each other. When a musician ran into health problems or financial difficulties, a fundraiser was organized, and all of these guys would show up, plus a host of other musicians. They were not solely business associates. They cared for each other.

I remember Johnny singing at a number of those fundraisers. When the call went out, he was there, ready to raise the roof for his friend in need. I have never before witnessed a bond quite like the one these musicians shared -- as strong as any biological family.

Johnny and I were shocked when we learned that we would need that same support ourselves.

When Johnny was diagnosed with cancer, he was given six months to live. However, in a very short period of time we had depleted our life savings, paying for medicine and oxygen machines that were not covered under our health insurance. It's amazing how a terminal illness can so quickly strip you of your financial assets. All of our money was spent on items to keep Johnny alive. If it was a choice between medication and groceries, money went for medication.

As debt was overwhelming us, the family of musicians silently stepped in to pick up the slack. They knew we needed help, but they knew Johnny was a proud man and would not ask for a hand out. He didn't have to ask. Fundraisers were immediately organized in New Orleans, and a host of musicians participated. The

Music Cares Foundation also stepped in and covered the cost of medical bills.

The hardest pill for Johnny to swallow during his illness was an emotional one. He knew that his albums were out there being sold on a daily basis. He had worked so hard and built a career through much personal sacrifice and long hours, days, and months away from home. But 7 cents an album doesn't go very far when you're fighting cancer. It was personally heartbreaking for him to need financial help at that point in his life and in his career.

As Johnny lay there, many musicians filled the room, as well as the hall each and every day. Family members, friends and many fans could not stay away from their fallen hero. But Johnny's hero was his Retired fire fighter brother, James. James Smith had flown down from California when I notified him of his brother's medical condition. While this may sound like a common labor of love which most family members would certainly do, what made it powerful was that Johnny's brother had recently suffered a stroke.

Under doctors care and heavy medication and advised not to travel, James, a hero to many Fire victims, was also a hero for his brother. Even with his own life at risk, he ignored that and hopped on the first flight her could to be with his brother.

I don't think the airplane could land fast enough for him. The heroism began when he arrived at our home. James rushed to his brother's bed side and catered to his every need. He fed Johnny, gave him water, helped change him. He would get up early in the morning and sit on the lounge chair in the living room. He would sit next to Johnny and talk to him for hours. He inspired my husband and kept him in good spirits. In the evenings he would walk Johnny to the bedroom and help get him into bed. I admire James so much because he seems to never get tired. The most touching moments was when he prayed with his brother. Seemed like the spirit would fill the whole house.

As Johnny's condition began to get worse, James seemed to get stronger. Later, Johnny was taken to "our lady of the lake" hospital were James continued to stay at his brothers side. I did become concerned for his health at times, but he wouldn't hear it. Like a fireman who's used to rescuing and saving lives, his wellbeing was always considered last. He was truly Johnny's hero. James remained by his brothers side until he passed away.

CHAPTER EIGHT

Please Release Me

But Johnny's spirits were lifted by the ongoing, never-ending support of his family of musicians. Aaron Neville visited Johnny in the hospital and called me almost daily to see how Johnny was doing. Walter "Wolfman" Washington, Johnny's band leader, was there for him. Pianist Ruth Brown, David Torkanowsky, Duke Robillard, Dr. John, Dr. Lonnie Smith, and Houston Person all came to help; the list of support goes on and on. There was a constant stream of visitors and phone calls and fundraisers building a wall of courage around Johnny's bed.

Listen to the recording Aaron Neville and Johnny made of "Never Alone" on the *Man of My Word* CD. The song brings tears to my eyes. I can hear the spiritual connection those men shared as their voices weave in and out of each other. Moments after Johnny took his last breath, Aaron called me. There was silence on the other end of the line when I told him the news. They shared a brotherhood, a respect, and a deep love for each other. Aaron was inconsolable at the funeral.

I will never forget what all of those musicians did for Johnny. I will always remember who showed up when the chips were down. It was the musicians – the performers – who stuck together through good times and bad. The musical family did what they do best – they loved each other and they helped each other.

I remember the day like it was yesterday. It was when Johnny went to the hospital for a series of testing. Testing for a hernia he developed while playing golf. His DR., Fredrick Billings, had completed all the testing.

DR. Billings entered the exam room with the results in hand and quickly began reading the test results to us. He explained that Johnny had prostate cancer and the cancer has spread throughout his body. Both of us were in shock and began asking many questions concerning the spread of the cancer. The DR. answered all our questions truthfully. But the bad news was, he had given Johnny less than one year to live. The Doctor suggested some different cancer treatments and then left the room. Johnny and I held each other tight as tears began to flow as an endless river. We no longer knew what tomorrow held for us… all we knew was we would embrace tomorrow together.

With my eyes swollen by tears, I began to reflect and consider not completing our journey through life together. We had become one and our souls were connected forever. I began to think about loosing him and how he wouldn't be there to help raise our little girl. He would never see her graduate from high school; he would not be there for college graduation. O lord he will not walk her down the wedding isle. he will never see his grand kids. It was almost too much for me to bear. Then Johnny said to me with over whelming sadness, "Sweetie, I don't want to leave you and the baby." I held him very close to me. Johnny said, "I know I told you to keep the media out, the newspapers, but if I die promise me you will tell my story…maybe even write a book. You will have no rest until you tell my story." I said I would.

As the weeks went buy Johnny began the cancer treatments at the hospital and he became very weak and spent most of his time confined to the house.

Before long, canisters of oxygen filled the room. Even the charm of DR Billing's bedside manners when he came to our home to care for Johnny could not warm up that cold bed. But he offered Johnny great conversation. I also had to become a total homebody staying by Johnny's bedside day after day and never leaving him alone. There was a nurse sent to the home on a daily bases to administer medication.

It was heart breaking to watch our home become a medical facility. It looked like a movie scene. I remember when our daughter would come home from school she would rush to daddy's room and climb up on the chair next to his bed and then climb in bed to hug and kiss him. Then she would lie down next to him and both of them would fall to sleep together. When Alitalia would later awake she would help feed her father and help him drink his water. Her job was to put the straw in the water or milk for him… she loved that. She

119

always had a soft towel to wipe off his mouth if he spilled a little…she was so sweet to her daddy. And always, she and Johnny would say their prayers before Alitalia went to bed.

CHAPTER NINE

Life Without Johnny

Where do I even begin to describe what life is now without my beloved husband by my side. In life we were soul mates and I feel that in death, we've become something even more…we've become a part of each other in ways I'd never imagined possible.

I'd like to take a moment and talk a little about the devastation caused by Hurricane Katrina. Remember, all of Johnny's brothers and sisters as well as his step-mother lived in New Orleans during that disaster and all of them lost their homes as well as future hopes the day Katrina took the last of their dreams and washed them out to sea.

It's truly been a heartbreaking time for Johnny's family and for me.

It was August 28th, 2005 when Hurricane Katrina slammed into the Southern coast of the United States with a devastating effect that would ripple on for years and years to come. It was reported that over 2,000 people lost their lives and over $81 billion dollars in damages occurred as a result of this natural disaster. By August 31st, 80% of New Orleans was flooded with some areas ending up over 15 feet under water. Johnny's brother, Edward, sister, Aurolan and stepmother, Edna Adams, were some of the fortunate ones who after three days on their rooftops and with only the clothes on their backs, were finally rescued and brought to safety. Johnny's stepmother, Edna, was flown to Lackland Air force base in Texas where she almost lost her life due to dehydration. As Edward recalled, he had created a hole in the floor of their home where he helped pull all his family members onto the roof saving all their lives. Edward was always very close to his brother, Johnny in fact, he attended just about every show Johnny ever performed in New Orleans.

I thank God that I was able to help Johnny's family by shipping them clothing in all their sizes. I was also able to help other victims of Katrina who happened to be long time friends of Johnny like Fat's Domino along with his daughter and grandchildren. They were all taken to a little town in Texas called, Plano. Fats Domino's daughter and Johnny's sister, Aurolan were great friends so when Aurolan contacted me and I got the clothing sizes for Fats, his wife, daughter and grandchildren, with the help of local churches, we were able to quickly acquire and send plenty of clothing to all our friends and family there in New Orleans. What a blessing it was to be able to help in that great time of need. As it ended up, we were able to help clothe over one hundred hurricane victims and with the help of several friends who were beauticians, I was also able to get free grooming for over another hundred flood victims. It was a great tribute to Johnny and he would have loved seeing his family and friends come together reaching out to all those in need and providing so much assistance.

But life without my beloved Johnny is very different and every day I sit down at my computer I realize that even after my dear husband's death, the record producers and money changers continue to rob him and our family.

One thing that continues to haunt me and the family of Johnny Adams is that fact that literally hundreds of web sites today sell thousands of Johnny's CD's each year and no family member has ever seen much money in royalties. Part of this could be because of the incorrect accounting practices, wrong invoices and lack of sales invoicing supplied by the companies in violation.

There are also the unauthorized photos of Johnny Adams used daily for which no compensation has ever been paid to his wife or estate.

It seems that the internet has made it very easy for producers and promoters to release music, pictures even unauthorized stories about Johnny Adams without ever compensating family members for their use…this has got to stop.

All this just seems to fuel the fires of grief that is still within me. The never ending sadness
that turns to grieving grief whenever I think about the final absence of the dearest part of my life. The swift and unexpected removal of my life long

partner…that passionate, but untouchable missing void in my life. An irreplaceable soul divided as an apple split through its middle to the very core.

But I suppose the fight will go on as the getting ripped off, even after the years of my husband passing, continues. And although the fight to recover record royalties may continue for a lifetime, I enjoy the comfort of knowing it's what Johnny would have wanted.

But I still can't help but be amazed by the things that are still taking place even after his death. Even with no payments from any of the early record companies, and very little from his last recording, several new CDs continue to be licensed and released. Some of those new releases have been coming out of Australia (aim Records) which had taken photos of Johnny from a performance many years prior to their release (the immortal soul of Johnny Adams) and is currently being sold in the United States and on several web sites.

Other Johnny Adams cds, where the covers of the cds have photos of Johnny, are ones that I have never seen. The massive number of cds sold has not been reported accurately or at all and there are large reporting differences made to me over the last few years.

I have received a second scan sales report recently that proves inaccurate accounting. Johnny's cds continue to have record breaking sales, and can be found selling on several web sites, yet neither I nor any of his family members are yet to be included in their profits.

Then there is the fight to get copies of the original contracts the record company claim they signed with Johnny, even though he was never allowed to have his own attorney present or even represent him. The justice I am still seeking for Johnny is the justice that all Americans enjoy…the justice in making things right based on the laws of the land. The justice for the many cds released after his death with no contact to Johnny's estate, or myself. The justice for the real ownership of the masters along with the release of several songs recorded in record studios. This done with no proven contracts and released after his death claiming they own the masters and can use his image, by placing there own personal photos on cds, and releasing them. The fight to get his civil right restored.

Johnny recorded 26 cds, and performed on 85 different recording artist cds, which included Harry Connic Jr. released in 1992. "Silky soul" released 9/17/1996 through the label "Easy disc" "Fanning Flame" in 1996 with Maria Mulder under the label "Telarc", Doctors Professors and queen released on 10/26/2004 along with many others.

For over ten years now Jay B. Ross & Associates have been actively representing the Johnny Adams estate. In all that time they have only managed to collect a small amount of back royalties…in fact the dollar figure is under $4,000.00 to date.

They have not yet been able to collect from any record companies selling Johnny's records out of the country. It seems to be almost impossible to collect much of the money that is due Johnny Adams.

And it's not that these aren't highly respected attorneys who are great at what they do. They've handled many well known artists including the likes of James Brown.

And then there was the Rhythm& Blues Foundation Tenth Annual Pioneer Awards where many were honored. Here is a list of some of those honorees:

Johnny Adams

Bill Pinckney & Original Drifter)

Barbara Lewis

Brenda Holloway

Barbara Lynn

Garnet Mimms

Johnny Moore

Joe Simon,

Charlie Thomas

Dee Dee Warwick

Mickey Baker

The host for his event was Smokey Robinson along with Ashford and Simpson, David Porter and Issac Hayes who were recognized song writers. Groups honored were Pattie Labelle and the Bluebelles, and the Manhattans.

This Gala event took place at the Sony Studios in Los Angeles. Through the Rhythm & Blues foundation Pioneer Awards, the Foundation honors the men and women who were so instrumental in creating this rich art form.

During this event, Mrs. Judy Adams received three standing ovations for her speech (the music industry is dressed in suits and licensed to steal. (don't walk) run and get legal representation). This speech by Judy Adams seemed to have a profound affect with several recording artist like Patti Labelle who invited me and my five year-old daughter, Alitalia to join her at her table. Shortly after being seated next to her she quickly sat Alitalia on her lap and smiled. The next table over from us sat Mary Wilson (original singer of the Supremes) who quickly came over to our table and congratulated me on my speech. I learned that night that she had just started an origination to fight for the rights of musicians which has continued throughout the years.

   After speaking with several of the honorees at this event, I was surprised and sadly heart broken to hear that they to had experienced the same bone chilling effects from the music industry that

Johnny and I had. Pattie Labelle was a real comfort to me and warned me to be strong as she offered her assistance if I should ever need her. I felt blessed that night knowing the musical family supported m, and was here for me if I needed them.

CHAPTER TEN

JOHNNY'S GREATEST LEGACY

His Songs

And without a doubt when we think of the legacy left by Johnny Adams, it's the music that Johnny will forever be remembered by. From that first hit he had back in 1959, "I won't cry" to his second in 1962, "A losing battle" (this record was written and produced by Mac Rebennack, better known as Dr John) there would have been no way to imagine at the time that these first two hits from Johnny Adams would in retrospect seem to describe and parallel his life and ultimately his death.

In later years, Adams would state that these first hits could have been a major springboard into national success if only the independent label which owned them had been prepared to negotiate with some of the major labels of the time, but that never occurred.

Over the course of the sixties and seventies, Johnny Adams would rack up a string of hits including the country favorite, "Release Me" in 1968. In 1969 he would follow that up with "Reconsider Me" and "I Can't be All Bad"

Johnny's audience grew when he began working with producer Scott Billington at Rounder Records in the early eighties. In 1984 Johnny recorded, "From the Heart which many believed was a turning point in his career and would secure his success for decades to come.

Johnny had the privilege to work with many talented and gifted artists over the years. Johnny would ultimately put together elegantly rendered tribute albums to legendary songwriters Doc Pomus and Percy Mayfield.

The legendary Doc Pomus found success as one of the finest white blues singers of the 1940s before becoming one of the greatest songwriters in the history of American popular music. The author of many of the most popular rock & roll songs of the 1960s, he composed "Save the Last Dance for Me,'' "This Magic Moment," "Sweets for My Sweet" and dozens of others, including Elvis Presley's "Viva Las Vegas" "Little Sister," and "(Marie's the Name) His Latest Flame."

Crippled by polio in his childhood, Pomus -- born Jerome Felder on June 27, 1925 in Brooklyn, New York -- became interested in singing blues and writing songs after hearing a Big Joe Turner record when he was 15; he played saxophone at the time, and after hearing Turner, blues music became his obsession. By the mid-'50s, after singing in a thousand blues clubs, Pomus came to a crossroads in his career: he was in his early 30s and decided he wanted to get married, but realizing he'd never support himself and a wife singing blues, he decided to become a songwriter. He then realized he needed a collaborator, and found one in his piano-playing partner for dozens of years, Mort Shuman.

Together, Pomus and Shuman wrote the words and music to such hits as "Little Sister," "Suspicion," "Can't Get Used to Losing You," "Surrender," "Viva Las Vegas" and many more. After securing their own office in the Brill Building, the team continued to crank out hit after hit; Presley alone ended up recording more than 20 of their songs throughout his career, including items like "Mess of Blues." In addition, Pomus and Shuman also wrote songs for Fabian ("Turn Me Loose" and "I'm a Man"), Bobby Darin ("Plain Jane") and

Dion, for whom they wrote "Teenager in Love."

Pomus worked tirelessly for singers he believed in, and among those he believed in was Little Jimmy Scott, a jazz balladeer from Cleveland who first came to New York in the late '40s as part of Lionel Hampton's band. He also played significant career boosting roles for people like his hero Big Joe Turner, Dr. John, Lou Reed and dozens of others.

Pomus contracted lung cancer and died in March 1991, but not before a string of benefit shows were held for him at clubs around New York; after Scott performed "Someone to Watch Over Me" at Pomus' memorial service, the singer was signed to a five album deal with Warner Bros. Pomus' memory lives on via the Washington, D.C.-based Rhythm and Blues Foundation's Doc Pomus Financial Assistance program.

A masterful songwriter whose touching blues ballad "Please Send Me Someone to

Love," a multi-layered universal lament, was a number one R&B hit in 1950, Percy Mayfield had the world by the tail until a horrific 1952 auto wreck left him facially disfigured. That didn't stop the poet laureate of the blues from writing in prolific fashion, though.

As Ray Charles's favorite scribe during the '60s, he handed the Genius such gems as "Hit the Road Jack" and "At the Club."

Like so many of his postwar L.A. contemporaries, Mayfield got his musical start in Texas but moved to the coast during the war. Surmising that Jimmy Witherspoon might like to perform a tune he'd penned called "Two Years of Torture," Mayfield targeted Supreme Records as a possible buyer for his song. But the bosses at Supreme liked his own gentle reading so much that they insisted he wax it himself in 1947 with an all-star band that included saxist Maxwell Davis, guitarist Chuck Norris, and pianist

Willard McDaniel.

Art Rupe's Specialty logo signed Mayfield in 1950 and he scored a solid string of R&B smashes over the next couple of years. "Please Send Me Someone to Love" and its equally potent flip "Strange Things Happening" were followed in the charts by "Lost Love," "What a Fool I Was," "Prayin' for Your Return," "Cry Baby," and "Big Question," cementing Mayfield's reputation as a blues balladeer of the highest order. Davis handled sax duties on most of Mayfield's Specialty sides as well. Mayfield's lyrics were usually as insightfully downbeat as his tempos; he was a true master at expressing his innermost feelings, laced with vulnerability and pathos (his "Life Is Suicide" and "The River's Invitation" are two prime examples).

Even though his touring was drastically curtailed after the accident, Mayfield hung in there as a Specialty artist through 1954, switching to Chess in 1955-56 and Imperial in 1959. Charles proved thankful enough for Mayfield's songwriting genius to sign him to his Tangerine logo in 1962; over the next five years, the singer waxed a series of inexorably classy outings, many with Brother Ray's band (notably "My Jug and I" in 1964 and "Give Me Time to Explain" the next year).

It's a rare veteran blues artist indeed who hasn't taken a whack at one or more Mayfield copyrights. Mayfield himself persisted into the '70s, scoring minor chart items for RCA and Atlantic while performing on a limited basis until his 1984 death.

Songwriter Dorothy Labostrie, the woman responsible for cleaning up the bawdy lyrics of Little Richard's "Tutti Frutti" enough for worldwide consumption -- convinced her neighbor, Johnny Adams, to sing her tasty ballad "I Won't Cry." The track, produced by a teenaged Mac Rebennack, was released on Joe Ruffino's Ric logo, and Adams was on his way. He waxed some outstanding follow-ups for Ric, notably "A Losing Battle" (the Rebennack-penned gem proved Adams' first national R&B hit in 1962) and "Life Is a Struggle."

After a prolonged dry spell, Adams resurfaced in 1968 with an impassioned R&B revival of Jimmy Heap's country standard "Release Me"

Despite several worthy SSS follow-ups ("I Can't Be All Bad" was another sizable seller), Adams never traversed those lofty commercial heights again (particularly disappointing was a short stay at Atlantic). But he found a new extended recording life at Rounder; his 1984 set, From the Heart, proved to the world that this Tan Canary could still chirp like a champ. With producer Scott Billington, he recorded some nine albums

for the label prior to his cancer-related
death on September 14, 1998.

A TAN NIGHTINGALE

1969

1. Release Me
2. You Made a New Man Out of Me
3. How Can I Prove I Love You
4. You Can Depend on Me
5. Real Live Livin' Hurtin' Man
6. I Won't Cry
7. Losing Battle
8. I Have No One 9. Love Me Now
10. Proud Woman
11. Reconsider Me
12. Something Worth Leaving For
13. Let Me Be Myself
14. It's Got to Be Something
15. Hell Yes, I Cheated

CHRISTMAS IN NEW ORLEANS
1975

1. Silent Night
2. O Little Town of Bethlehem
3. The Lord's Prayer
4. Silver Bells
5. The Christmas Song
6. The Little Boy That Santa Forgot
7. This Christmas
8. Lonesome Christmas
9. The Bells of St. Mary's
10. White Christmas
11. Please Come Home for Christmas

RECONSIDER ME

1976

1. Reconsider Me

2. You Can Depend on Me

3. Kiss the Hurt Away

4. I Won't Cry

5. Proud Woman

6. The Tender Side of Me

7. Release Me

8. Too Much Pride

9. Real Live Livin' Hurtin' Man

10. If I Could See You One More Time

11. I Can't Be All Bad

12. In a Moment of Weakness

13. I Don't Worry Myself

14. You Made a New Man Out of Me

15. Down by the River

16. Lonely Man

17. I Have No One

18. A Losing Battle

Stand By Me

1976

FROM THE HEART

1984

1. I Feel Like Breaking Up Somebody's Home

2. Why Do I?

3. Laughing and Clowning

4. If I Ever Had a Good Thing

5. Scarred Knees

6. From the Heart

7. Your Love Is So Doggone Good

8. We Don't See Eye to Eye

9. Road Block

10. Teach Me to Forget

AFTER DARK

1985

1. Lovers Will
2. I Don't Know You
3. Fortune Teller
4. Missing You
5. Do Right Woman, Do Right Man
6. Give a Broken Heart a Break
7. She Said the Same Things to Me
8. Garbage Man
9. Dancing Man
10. Snap Your Fingers

ROOM WITH A VIEW OF THE BLUES

1987

1. Room With a View
2. I Don't Want to Do Wrong
3. Not Trustworthy (A Lyin' Woman)
4. Neither One of Us (Wants to Be the First to Say Goodbye)
5. How Wrong Can a Good Man Be
6. Body and Fender Man
7. I Owe You
8. Wish I'd Never Loved You at All
9. The Hunt Is On
10. A World I Never Made

WALKING ON A TIGHTROPE

1989

1. Walking on a Tightrope

2. Lost Mind

3. Stand By

4. My Heart Is Hangin' Heavy

5. Danger Zone

6. Never No More

7. The Lover and the Married Woman

8. You're in for a Big Surprise

9. Look the Whole World Over

10. Baby Please

THE REAL ME

1991

1. Imitation of Love

2. Still in Love

3. There Is Always One More Time

4. My Baby's Quit Me

5. She's Everything to Me

6. I Underestimated You

7. Blinded by Love

8. Prisoner of Life

9. The Night Is a Hunter

10. No One

11. The Real Me

I WON'T CRY

1991

1. (Oh Why) I Won't Cry
2. Life Is a Struggle
3. A Losing Battle
4. Nowhere to Go
5. Oh, So Nice
6. I Want to (Do Everything for You)
7. You Can Make It If You Try
8. Teach Me to Forget
9. Let the Winds Blow
10. I Solemnly Promise
11. Who Are You
12. Come On
13. Someone for Me
14. Lonely Drifter

JOHNNY ADAMS GREATEST PERFORMANCES
1993

1. Performance
2. Feeling
3. After All the Good Is Done
4. The Greatest Love
5. A Shoulder to Cry On
6. Love Me Tender
7. Oh Yes I Cheated
8. Closer to You
9. Sharing You
10. It's You Baby, It's You
11. Baby I'm-a-Want You
12. Feel the Beat
13. Stairway to Heaven
14. Love Letters
15. Best of Luck to You
16. Think About You
17. Struttin' on Sunday
18. Turning Point

GOOD MORNING HEARTACHE

1993

1. You Don't Know What Love Is

2. I Just Found Out About Love

3. Don't Go to Strangers

4. Jealous Kind

5. I Hadn't Anyone Till You

6. Come Rain or Come Shine

7. Teach Me Tonight

8. Good Morning Heartache

9. Back to Normal

10. But Not for Me

JOHNNY ADAMS BEST OF NEW ORLEANS RHYTHM & BLUES

VOLUME 1

1995

1. Tell It Like It Is

2. Who Will the Next Fool Be?

3. Stay With Me

4. Hell Yes, I Cheated

5. Baby I Love You

6. I'll Never Fall in Love Again

7. Your Love Is All I Need

8. Share Your Love With Me

9. Don't Let the Green Grass Fool You

10. Nothing Takes the Place of You

11. Give Me a Chance

12. I Only Want to Be With You

13. Love Me Now

14. One Fine Day

15. Stand by Me

16. Our Day Will Come

17. Spanish Harlem

THE VERDICT

1995

1. Blue Gardenia

2. The Verdict

3. City Lights

4. Dreams Must Be Going Out of Style

5. Down That Lonely Lonely Road

6. I Cover the Waterfront

7. Love for Sale

8. You Always Knew Me Better

9. A Lot of Living to Do

10. Willow Weep for Me

11. Come Home to Love

12. D Jam Blues

ONE FOOT IN THE BLUES

1996

1. Won't Pass Me By

2. One Foot in the Blues

3. Baby Don't You Cry

4. Ill Wind

5. Road Block

6. Angel Eyes

7. Half Awake (Baby, You're Still a Square)

8. (I Wonder) Where Our Love Has Gone

9. Two Years Of Torture

10. Cookin' In Style

11. I Know What I've Got

MAN OF MY WORD

1998

1. Even Now

2. It Ain't the Same Thing

3. This Time I'm Gone for Good

4. Going Out of Mind Sale

5. Now You Know

6. Up and Down World

7. I Don't Want to Know 8. Man of My Word

9. You Don't Miss Your Water

10. Bulldog Break His Chain

11. It Tears Me Up

12. Looking Back

13. Never Alone

THE IMMORTAL SOUL OF JOHNNY ADAMS

1999

1. I Only Wanna Be With You
2. I'll Never Fall in Love Again
3. Love Me Now
4. Stairway to Heaven
5. Give Me a Chance
6. Turning Point
7. Who Will the Next Fool Be
8. Your Love Is All I Need
9. Stay With Me
10. Share Your Love
11. Closer to You
12. Sharing With You
13. Think About You
14. Don't Let the Green Grass Fool You
15. Spanish Harlem

THERE IS ALWAYS ONE MORE TIME
2000

1. I Feel Like Breaking up Somebody's Home

2. Happy Hard Times

3. I'll Only Miss Her When I Think of Her

4. I Don't Know

5. Lovers Will

6. One Foot in the Blues

7. Even Now

8. Body and Fender Man

9. There Is Always One More Time

10. Walking on a Tightrope

11. Don't Want to Do Wrong

12. A Lot of Living to Do

13. Wish I'd Never Loved You at All

14. But Not for Me

15. Never Alone

JOHNNY ADAMS MEMORIAL ALBUM

2001

1. Release Me
2. You Made a New Man Out of Me
3. I Won't Cry
4. In a Moment of Weakness
5. I Want to Walk Through This Life With You
6. Reconsider Me
7. If I Could See You One More Time
8. South Side of Soul Street
9. Georgia Morning Dew
10. Real Live Livin' Hurtin' Man
11. Lonely Man
12. Proud Woman
13. Losing Battle
14. How Can I Prove I Love You
15. You Can Depend on Me
16. Let Me Be Myself
17. It's Got to Be Something
18. Share Your Love With Me
19. Your Love Is All I Need
20. Stairway to Heaven

21. After All the Good Is Gone

22. Chasing Rainbows

23. Love Me Now

24. Hell Yes I Cheated

ABSOLUTELY THE BEST

2002

1. I Won't Cry

2. I Can't Be All Bad

3. Release Me

4. Reconsider Me

5. You Made a New Man Out of Me

6. In a Moment of Weakness

7. I Want to Walk Through This Life With You

8. If I Could See You One More Time

9. South Side of Soul Street

10. Georgia Morning Dew

11. Real Live Living Hurtin' Man

12. Lonely Man

13. Proud Woman

14. A Losing Battle

15. How Can I Prove I Love You

16. The Tender Side of Me

17. Kiss the Hurt Away

18. You Can Depend on Me

THE GREAT JOHNNY ADAMS BLUES ALBUM
2005

1. Not Trustworthy (A Lyin' Woman)

2. My Heart Is Hangin' Heavy

3. Laughin' and Clownin'

4. Danger Zone

5. Imitation of Love

6. Garbage Man

7. Roadblock

8. Scarred Knees

9. Fortune Teller

10. Room with a View

11. My Baby's Quit Me

12. This Time I'm Gone for Good

THE GREAT JOHNNY ADAMS R&B ALBUM

2006

1. I Need a Lot of Loving

2. From the Heart

3. You Don't Miss Your Water

4. She Said the Same Things to Me

5. I Feel Like Breaking Up Sombody's Home

6. She's Everything to Me

7. Neither One of Us (Wants to Be the First to Say Goodbye)

8. Going Out of My Mind Sale

9. The Jealous Kind

10. If I Ever Had a Good Thing

11. Won't Pass Me By

12. Still in Love

AN INTRODUCTION TO JOHNNY ADAMS
2006

1. After All the Good Is Gone
2. The Best of Luck to You
3. Don't Let the Green Grass Fool You
4. Your Love Is All I Need
5. A Shoulder to Cry On
6. Who Will the Next Fool Be
7. Hell Yes I Cheated
8. I Only Want to Be with You
9. Give Me a Chance
10. Share Your Love with Me
11. Struttin' on Sunday
12. I'll Never Fall in Love Again
13. Love Letters
14. Thinking About You
15. Love Me Now
16. Sharing You

The Tan Canary

New Orleans Soul – 1973-1981

Released 2007

1. After All the Good Is Gone

2. Somewhere

3. Selfish

4 . She's Only a Baby Herself

5 . Chasing Rainbows

6 . I Can't Believe She Gives It All to Me

7 . The Image of Me

8 . Stay with Me and Stay in Love

9 . One Fine Day

10 . It's Been So Long

11 . Spanish Harlem

12 . It's Got to Be Something

13 . It Only Rains on Me

14 . Night People

15 . Memories

16 . Put It off Till Tomorrow

17 . Baby, Baby I Love You

18 . Don't Let the Green Grass Fool You

19 . Give Me a Chance

20 . I Don't Wanna Cry

21 . I'll Never Fall in Love Again

22 . Nothing Takes the Place of You

23 . Share Your Love with Me

24 . Who Will the Next Fool Be

25 . Your Love Is All I Need

26 . Stand by Me

27 . Bells of St. Mary

28 . White Christmas

29 . I Can't Be All Bad

30 . Too Much Pride

31 . Born to Love You

32 . Just Call Me Darling

Below are the original recordings that Joe Ruffino, and the teenage Mac Rebennack, now known as (Dr. John), claimed to have signed with Johnny Adams, and released, and now then were re-released in 1991 and produced by Jeff Hannusch.

No where to go

Oh So Nice

I Want to Do Everything for You

You Can Make It if you Try

Teach Me to Forget.

Let the wind Blow

I Somely Promise

Who Are You

Come on

Someone for Me

Last Lonely Drifter

Johnny Adams' (Chasing Rainbows CD) The tan Canary New Orleans soul 1969-1981 recordings these recordings were released through the period of the years 1969 through 1981 and these early recordings on this CD were recorded in New Orleans by Senator Jones at the Sea Saint Studios mainly during the late 1970s.

Most of these recordings were found on labels, such as Chelsea records, Ariola, Hep, records of New Orleans owner, Senator Jones, and SSS international, all small town labels. These songs were released in this order:
"After all the Good is Gone" followed by "Somewhere selfish" from Senator Johns New Orleans "Help Me label"

There were also several cuts from the SSS label. Interestingly, the photo on the CD cover is the same photo used from the movie, "The Bird" which Johnny stared in as the bar tender. The issue on the use of this photo is part of my on-going legal battles since they do not have permission for the use or the right to use his image at all with out my written consent. This of course, is just one more injustice done to my husband, Johnny.

The CD was released by Shout Records and distributed by cherry records ltd located in the UK. This makes it very difficult to collect any royalties. There were also no upfront monies paid to Johnny's estate for the use of any of his photos, images or even his name. Bottom line, there was never a contact entered into from this record company when the record was released and distributed in the United States.

Johnny Adams' CD"The Great Johnny Adams Blues Album" was released in 2005 by Rounder records with producer Scott Billington, and co-producer Mac Rebennack (known as DR. John) The album is described by many as "Great" not only because of its large amount of sales it did, but because of the first rate cast of musicians performing on this classy R&B CD.

The opening song (Not Trustworthy) features Johnny Adams as vocal, guitar player Duke Robillard, his famous New Orleans band leader Walter (Wolfman Washington) Mac Rebennack (DR. John) world class bass player, David Berard and features Herman Earnest on drums. This song was featured from Johnny previous rounder record CD entitled, "Room With A View Of the blues" which has also sold thousands of copies. The next song on this CD (My Heart Is Hanging Heavy) is a Percy Mayfield song that Johnny pays tribute to.

The track includes Johnny as lead vocal, Duke Robillard as Lead guitar player, Band leader, Walter Washington as lead guitar along with the world renown piano player, John Cleary, the blues machine acoustic, James Singleton and on drums Johnny Vidacovich.

We believed nothing could top this until the next song from this CD,"Laughin and clowning" (SAM Cook) recording brought in even more great performers like Craig Wroten on piano and organ. You can here a class act with Darrel Francis, SR on bass and get your ears ready for Alvin (Red) Tyler on tenor saxophone. Then you can feel the excitement coming from Bill Samuel on baritone saxophone. And then last but not least, you'll hear sounds that make you think of angels in flight when listening to Terry Tulliou on trumpet.

This group made the song "Laughin and clowning" whisper to the world with a joyful noise. The next song would pull even harder and rope the talents of world famous John Cleary on piano to this eye opening song (Danger Zone) joining John is James Singleton Acoustic Bass, Johnny Vidacovich on drums, and of course Johnny is vocals on all the songs.

"Danger zone" is also a Percy Mayfield song (Imitation Of love) Doc Pomus Mac Rebennack and Stazybo music-skull music, BMI includes Johnny Adams as lead vocal, with Mac Rebennack on piano Duke Robillard on guitar, James Singleton on acoustic bass, Johnny Vidacovich on drums and Eric Traub would join them. Then on tenor saxophone showing his sophisticated style on baritone is Alvin Red Tyler. Also joining this fantastic group of musicians on trumpet, Charlie Miller. This cast certainly paid tribute to the very loved and remembered R&B doctrine of music. Doc Pomus was a long time and respected friend of Johnny.

The song (Garbage Man) is one of Johnny's New Orleans fans best loved song. This song can be found on the Johnny After Dark CD which is also on rounder Records. Johnny shows off not only his vocal talents, but surprises his large fan base around the world with his playing lead guitar and what a great guitar player he was. His playing can also be found on some of his other recordings.

Joining Johnny on rhythm guitar is, Elijah Rogers and on piano, Craig Wroten. Darrell Francis also joins Johnny showing off his talents on bass and Wilbert Arnold on drums. This song was taken from the After dark album, which had great sales success over seas as well as the other thirteen CD's released by rounder Records. This CD seems to reach more blues fans in France and Japan.

Johnny has always and continues to have a large fan base out of the country that enjoyed this CD as well as (walking On A Tight Rope)

The seventh song on this collectible album released by Rounder Records, "The Great Johnny Adams Blues Album" is (road Block My Baby (L.J. Welch/Cynthia music, BMI) joining Johnny on this song is DR. Lonnie Smith performing on a Hammond B3 organ as well as new comer, Jimmy Ponder on guitar. Donald Harrison jr. was playing alto saxophone ED Petersen on tenor saxophone and Shannon Powell on drums. This song can be found on still another of Johnny's CDs (One Foot In The Blues) also recorded on Rounder Records.

Road Block has been featured and played numerous times on the local New Orleans Radio Station WWOZ and is one of Johnny's favorites. It's continually played around New Orleans Blues clubs and radio stations throughout the Southern states.

Song number eight on this CD (scared Knees) Johnny is the lead vocal and this song is featured from his hit CD," From the heart" also on Rounder Records, "Scarred knees" (Janis Tyrone/Liletta music, BMI) features Johnny vocal Walter Washington on guitar, Craig Wroten on piano and on organ, Darrel Francis, SR.

Joining them on base was George Geeje Jackson jr. and on congas Wilbert Arnold.

Clearly, Johnny was surrounded by some of the most gifted and talented musicians in New Orleans, and from all over the world.

Johnny's music had no racial barriers, but he used his music to unite many different multi culture musicians to silently break the racial barriers that did exist in the music industry. This was Johnny's silent march for African American musicians who would have not been given a chance to present their musical talents to the world if Johnny would have not been able to become successful in the integrated market.

Johnny was able to enter and open doors in New Orleans as well as other Southern music markets that most African American musicians were never able to do.

The next song on the CD, "Road Block" L. J. Welch - Cynthia Music, BMI comes from Johnny's earlier CD released on Rounder Records "One Foot In The Blues" in which Johnny is vocal and DR. Lonnie Smith is on the Hammond b3 organ. Jimmy Ponder is on guitar, Donald Harrison alto saxophone, Ed Peterson on tenor saxophone and Shannon Powell on the drums. This song is on Johnny's CD "One Foot In The Blues" recorded on Rounder Records.

The next song "Scarred Knees" (Janis Tyrone/Liletta Music. BMI) will find Johnny as the vocal, Johnny's Band leader, Walter Washington is on guitar followed by Craig Wroten on piano and on the organ is Darrel Francis. On bass is George Jackson on congo and Wilbert Arnold on drums.

This song was recorded on Johnny Album "From The Heart" also recorded by Scott Billington on the Rounder record label.

The From the Heart album was a very intense album as well as very emotional album for Johnny because this album tells of Johnny's heart and the inner emotion Johnny was feeling at that time.

Several of the songs from that album seemed to be all about what Johnny was living at that time and some of the things going on in his life.

Song nine would surprise his fans with even more of Johnny's talents. In this song he shocks his fans around the world with his song writing ability. Many were surprised to learn that Johnny had written several songs including this one "fortune teller" (Johnny Adams/Happy Valley Music BMI) this song is also on an earlier released (After Dark) CD.

Once again on the Rounder Record label Johnny shows off his incredible writing talents that gives and sets the tone to this smooth, soulful tender ballard...it's truly amazing.

The last song on this album "Room With A View Of The Blues" was re-recorded from the "Room With A view" CD (Lowell Fulson-

Billy Vera/Arc Music Corp- Vera Cruz
Music, Ascap Administered by Warner
Brothers Music Corp) an interview and a
video of Johnny was shot by local
television station channel nine by the
late Vernon R. This was an incredible
video that captured Johnny in his finest
crooning performance.

The next song on this album "my Baby
Quit me" (Doc Pomus-Joe/Stazybo Music-
Meager Music, BMI) has Johnny on vocals
Mac on piano, Duke Robillard on guitar,
James Singleton on acoustic bass Johnny
Vidacovich on drums, Eric Traub tenor
saxophone, Alvin Red Tyler on baritone
saxophone and Charles Miller on Trumpet.
Even more talented musicians would join
Johnny to make this album what the title
indicates GREAT!

This CD mixture seems to capture
Johnny's talents as well as what he, as a
legendary recording artist, has offered
and given to his fans, his musical family

and the world. He has left his great classic smooth crooning, his soul, ballard, his honey voice, his soul gripping shouts, and his tender sophisticated tones.

Not only in this collection of songs but his life of songs and the music he gave to the world.

The last and final song on this album will give an ever lasting chill to the world and his fans, as well as myself. This song "This Time I'm Gone For Good" was the last song Johnny would give the world. This song comes from the Last CD Johnny recorded before his unforeseen death. This song was re-recorded from the "Man Of MY Word" CD, the last CD he recorded from Rounder Records.

This song "This time I'm Gone For Good" (Oscar Lee Perry-Deadric Malone/MCA Duchess Music Corp. BMI) is a ghostly and almost chilling to the bones song of Johnny telling the world he was leaving this place for good. You can here him smoothly convey the message and almost see him leaving this musical grave on earth, crooning his way into his beacon call onto the other side.

In every aching breath he sang in this song he was crooning to the final trumpet and triumph of his life.

Below is a list of Johnny Adams' credits over the years. As you can see, this great artist was involved with making many wonderful memories in a number of different ways.

- Various Artists
- City of Dreams: A Collection of New Orleans Music
- Vocals
- Various Artists
- Celebration of New Orleans Music to Benefit the Musicares Hurricane Relief
- Vocals
- Various Artists

- Doctors, Professors, Kings and Queens: The Big Ol' Box of New Orleans
- Vocals
- Various Artists
- Stepping Up
- Trombone
- Various Artists
- Gospel Brunch Classics
- Vocals
- Various Artists
- Box of the Blues
- Vocals
- Otis Grand
- Live Anthology
- Group Member
- Otis Grand
- Live Anthology
- Trumpet
- Various Artists
- Roots Music: An American Journey
- Vocals
- Various Artists
- For Connoisseurs Only

- Performer
- Steve Wilkerson
- Licorice Ice
- Liner Notes
- Larry McKenna
- It Might As Well Be Spring
- Liner Notes
- Various Artists
- Winter Memories (Definitive)
- Performer
- Various Artists
- Soulful Christmas (Definitive)
- Performer
- Various Artists
- Winter Wonderland (Definitive)
- Performer
- Various Artists
- New Orleans Soul '60s: Watch Records
- Performer
- Various Artists
- Louisiana Gumbo
- Performer
- Various Artists

- George Goldner Presents The Gone Story: Doo-Wop to Soul 1957-1963
- Performer
- Various Artists
- 20 Year Anniversary Celebration: Life's a Beach 1979-1999
- Performer
- David Newman
- Bowfinger
- Performer
- Various Artists
- Essential Blues, Vol. 3
- Performer
- Various Artists
- Essential Blues, Vol. 3
- Vocals
- Various Artists
- Dave Godin's Deep Soul Treasures: Taken From Our Vaults, Vol. 2
- Performer
- Various Artists
- Whole Lotta Soul 1968-1969
- Performer

- Various Artists
- Southern Soul Brothers (Waldoxy)
- Performer
- Various Artists
- One Nation Under Blues: Modern Masters 1980's
- Performer
- Various Artists
- Blue Christmas (Delta)
- Performer
- Various Artists
- Blues Masters, Vol. 17: More Postmodern Blues
- Performer
- Various Artists
- Blues Masters, Vol. 17: More Postmodern Blues
- Vocals
- Various Artists
- Modern New Orleans Masters
- Vocals
- Various Artists
- New Orleans Hit Story

- Performer
- Various Artists
- Blues Cruise: Ten for the Highway
- Performer
- Various Artists
- Merry Christmas (Golden Sounds)
- Performer
- Various Artists
- Blues Cruise: Ten for the Highway
- Vocals
- Various Artists
- Jumpin' the Blues, Vol. 1
- Performer
- Various Artists
- Tighten Up: No. 1 Soul Hits of the 60's, Vol. 2
- Performer
- Various Artists
- New Blues Hits
- Performer
- Various Artists
- New Blues Hits
- Vocals

- Ruth Brown
- R+B = Ruth Brown
- Vocals
- Various Artists
- Silky Soul
- Performer
- Various Artists
- Soul After Hours
- Various Artists
- Soul After Hours
- Performer
- Various Artists
- Great Holiday Classics With Christmas All-stars
- Performer
- Maria Muldaur
- Fanning the Flames
- Vocals
- The Embers
- Let's Have a Party!
- Performer
- Various Artists
- This Is Soul, Vol. 2 (Charly)

- Performer
- Various Artists
- Boogie Beat, Vol. 1
- Performer
- The New Orleans C.A.C. Orchestra
- Mood Indigo
- Performer
- The New Orleans C.A.C. Orchestra
- Mood Indigo
- Vocals
- Various Artists
- Soul Patrol, Vol. 3
- Performer
- Various Artists
- Legendary R&B & Blues, Vol. 1 (Black Tiger)
- Performer
- Various Artists
- Inner City Blues: The Music of Marvin Gaye
- Keyboards
- Various Artists

- Inner City Blues: The Music of Marvin Gaye
- Vocals
- Various Artists
- Rounder Records 25th Anniversary
- Performer
- Various Artists
- Louisiana Spice
- Performer
- Various Artists
- Louisiana Spice
- Vocals
- Various Artists
- Louisiana Spice
- Whistle (Human)
- Various Artists
- Soul Patrol, Vol. 2
- Various Artists
- Soul Patrol, Vol. 2
- Performer
- Various Artists
- American R&B Hits, Vol. 1 (Feelin' Good)

- Performer
- Various Artists
- Grits & Grooves
- Performer
- Various Artists
- Beach Beat Classics, Vol. 3
- Performer
- Various Artists
- Ebb Tide, Vol. 2
- Performer
- Various Artists
- Shagger's Delight, Vol. 5
- Performer
- Various Artists
- Soul of Christmas, Vol. 1
- Performer
- Various Artists
- Women of Gospel's Golden Age, Vol. 1
- Vocals (Background)
- Various Artists
- Still Spicy Gumbo Stew
- Performer
- Various Artists

- Soul of Christmas, Vol. 2
- Performer
- Various Artists
- Soul of Christmas, Vol. 2
- Vocals
- Various Artists
- Best of Louisiana Music (Mardi Gras 1993)
- Performer
- Various Artists
- Best of Louisiana Music (Rounder)
- Performer
- Various Artists
- More Gumbo Stew
- Performer
- Various Artists
- Blues Across the U.S.A.
- Vocals
- Various Artists
- Love Gets Strange: The Songs of John Hiatt
- Performer
- Various Artists

- Blues Across the U.S.A.
- Performer
- Harry Connick, Jr.
- 25
- Vocals
- Various Artists
- Soul Gold, Vol. 1
- Performer
- Various Artists
- Jewels, Vol. 2
- Performer
- Various Artists
- Sanctified: Gospel from New Orleans (Tititina's)
- Performer
- Various Artists
- Rhythm & Blues: 1969
- Performer
- Ray Rivera
- Night Wind
- Guitar
- Various Artists
- Modern New Orleans

- Performer
- Wynton Marsalis
- Tune in Tommorrow: Soundtrack
- Vocals
- Various Artists
- Classic Rock: On the Soul Side
- Performer
- Various Artists
- Rock 'N' Roll Era: The New Orleans Sound
- Performer
- Various Artists
- Creole Christmas
- Performer
- Wynton Marsalis
- Original Soundtrack from "Tune in Tomorrow"
- Performer
- Wynton Marsalis
- Original Soundtrack from "Tune in Tomorrow"
- Vocals
- Jeff Linsky

- Up Late
- Liner Notes
- Various Artists
- Carnival Time: The Best of Ric Records, Vol. 1
- Performer
- Various Artists
- Soul of New Orleans
- Performer
- Various Artists
- Carnival Time: The Best of Ric Records, Vol. 1
- Vocals
- Jack Sheldon
- Hollywood Heroes
- Liner Notes
- Various Artists
- Louisiana Scrapbook
- Various Artists
- Louisiana Scrapbook
- Mouth Trombone
- Various Artists
- History of New Orleans R&B, Vol. 3

- Performer
- Various Artists
- Steal This Disc
- Vocals
- Various Artists
- Steal This Disc
- Performer
- Various Artists
- Louisiana Scrapbook
- Vocals
- Various Artists
- Louisiana Scrapbook
- Performer
- Alvin "Red" Tyler
- Heritage
- Performer
- John Hunter
- More than Meets the Eye
- Singer
- Alvin "Red" Tyler
- Heritage
- Vocals
- Various Artists

- Out of the Blue (Rykodisc)
- Performer
- Various Artists
- Lost in the Stars: The Music of Kurt Weill
- Performer
- Various Artists
- Lost in the Stars: The Music of Kurt Weill
- Vocals
- Various Artists
- Out of the Blue (Rykodisc)
- Vocals
- Doggerel Bank
- Mister Skillcorn Dances
- Vocals
- Virgil Gonsalves
- Jazz at Monterey
- Liner Notes

And still more music from Johnny. Below are a number of albums that Johnny Adams appeared on. Some are from here in the states and many are from markets spanning the globe. Clearly, Johnny's music transcended country boarders as well as generations.

A Soulful Christmas (1999)

Best Of Louisiana Music! (2005)

Best Of Louisiana Music Sampler (1995)

Blues Across the U.S.A. (1993)

Blues In The Night (2004)

Box Of The Blues (2003)

Carnival Time: The Best Of Ric Records Vol. 1 (1988)

City Of Dreams: A Collection Of New Orleans Music (2007)

Doctors, Professors, Kings & Queens: The Big Ol' Box Of New Orleans (2004)

Fanning The Flames (1996)

Ghetto Funk Sessions (2004)

Gospel Brunch Classics (2003)

Hard To Find 45S On CD: Sweet Soul Sounds (2004)

Louisiana Spice: 25 Years Of Louisiana Music On Rounder Records (1995)

Merry Blue Christmas   (2002)

Modern New Orleans Masters   (1999)

Mood Indigo   (1997)

Music For Lovers   (2000)

New Blues Hits   (1997)

New Orleans Soul '60'S Watch
Records   (2000)

Night Train To Nashville Music City Rhythm
& Blues 1945-1970   (2004)

R+B = Ruth Brown   (1997)

Roots Music: An American Journey   (2001)

Rounder Records: A Celebration Of New
Orleans Music To Benefit The Musicares
Hurricane Relief Fund   (2004)

Senator Jones Funky New Orleans   (2005)

Shake What You Brought! The SSS Soul
Collection   (2005)

Silky Soul   (1996)

Soul After Hours   (1996)

Soul Of The Night   (2004)

The Real Music Box: 25 Years of Rounder
Records   (1995)

Ultimate New Orleans   (2005)

Wardell Quezerque's Funky New
Orleans (2005)

Blue Christmas

20 Songs For Christmas

A Holiday R&B Christmas (2005)

Christmas Box

Christmas Greatest

Christmas Legends

Christmas Party Time (2001)

Christmas Spectacular

Dirty Laundry: The Soul Of Black Country

Gospel Christmas

Jingle Bells

Le Plaisir

More Gumbo Stew

Our Turn To Cry (2001)

Silent Night

Singing The Blues: 44 Blues Classics

Soul Legends Vol. 2-Soul Legends

Soul Of Black

Soul: For Your Precious Love

Soul: I Will Survive

Southern Soul Showcase (2005)

Still Spicy Gumbo Stew (1995)

Supa Funka Nova

We Wish You A Merry

Wonderful Christmas

A FINAL THOUGHT

After his God and his family, Johnny's life was his music… and of course his fellow musicians, the ones who performed with him live and on the CDs, were considered to be just like family.

One song that related to Johnny's life in a big way is, "My Heart is hanging heavy" this song portrays a broken man who lives with great heartache. A kind of heartache that no other man could ever feel unless they had gone through some of the same great injustices that Johnny had experienced as a young black man growing up in the South. A young black man trying desperately to break free from the crippling hold the record companies had on his life.

The song "Laughin and clowning" seemed to give him some relief at times and spending time with his fellow musicians is what kept Johnny's sprit alive and together.

"Room with a View Of the Blues" seems to have been Johnny looking through the view of a window of his blues career. It was about having a vision that was larger then New Orleans and bigger than the local and small time record labels. It was also a view of his eternal life and a clear view of his calling and his mission from God...that mission; to complete his work in the music field and allow it to open new doors and of course to later tell his story to the world in the form or a book. It's why I'm writing this book today. Johnny's life has and will enrich forever. This was Johnny's life and his story and it continues long after his death.

This book is dedicated to our daughter Alitalia Adams

ACKNOWLEDGMENTS

- Offbeat magazine
- WWOZ Radio Station New Orleans
- WXOK radio station in Baton Rouge La
- All the radio stations through out the country who continue to keep Johnny music alive
- New Orleans Jazz fest owner Quint Davis for continuing to schedule Johnny to perform every year, allowing fans from all over the country to here his music for the first time.
- Rocking Doopsie
- Frankie Fordwarren Storm
- Tommy McClain
- Lil Alfred (The Boogie Kings T K Hulin the rascals
- The Louisiana Rock and Roll Hall of Fame that inducted him.
- Southern musical family

- Thanks to my friend Maxine Porter (manager of Bill Pinckney the Original Drifters) for writing an article about me in her book title (drifters 1)

- Mary Wilson (of the Supremes) has been fighting together for the injustices for older recording artist rights from the early 50s & 60s the Do Wop area.

- Rhythm & Blues foundation

- Music care Organization (several of the musician
  that helped Johnny at the must needed time of his last days)

- Adolph L. Reed Jr. (Johnny's friend, who acknowledge Johnny in his book W.E.B.)
  Du Bois and American Political Thought Fabianism, and the Color Line.

- His mother Mary Meyers, father Laten John Adams SR. brothers, and sisters.

Contact Information

Email: info@johnnyadams.org

Website: http://www.johnnyadams.org

www.ingramcontent.com/pod-product-compliance
Lightning Source LLC
Chambersburg PA
CBHW031254090426
42742CB00007B/449